INSTANT Piano Songs

Audio Access
Included

SONGS FOR KIDS
Simple Sheet Music + Audio Play-Along

T0057842

PLAYBACK+
Speed • Pitch • Balance • Loop

To access audio visit:
www.halleonard.com/mylibrary

Enter Code
1624-6601-8023-9081

ISBN 978-1-5400-7087-6

HAL•LEONARD®

Visit Hal Leonard Online at
www.halleonard.com

Contact us:
Hal Leonard
7777 West Bluemound Road
Milwaukee, WI 53213
Email: info@halleonard.com

In Europe, contact:
Hal Leonard Europe Limited
42 Wigmore Street
Marylebone, London, W1U 2RN
Email: info@halleonardeurope.com

In Australia, contact:
Hal Leonard Australia Pty. Ltd.
4 Lentara Court
Cheltenham, Victoria, 3192 Australia
Email: info@halleonard.com.au

CONTENTS

Welcome to the *INSTANT Piano Songs* series!

This unique, flexible collection allows you to play with either one hand or two. Three playing options are available—all of which sound great with the online backing tracks:

1. **Play only the melody with your right hand.**

2. **Add basic chords in your left hand, which are notated for you.**

3. **Use suggested rhythm patterns for the left-hand chords.**

Letter names appear inside the notes in both hands to assist you, and there are no key signatures to worry about. If a **sharp** ♯ or **flat** ♭ is needed, it is shown beside the note each time, even within the same measure.

If two notes are connected by a **tie** ‿, hold the first note for the combined number of beats. (The second note does not show a letter name since it is not re-struck.)

Sometimes the melody needs to be played an octave higher to avoid overlapping with the left-hand chords. (If your starting note is C, the next C to the right is one octave higher.) If you are using only your right hand, however, you can disregard this instruction in the music.

🔊 The backing tracks are designed to enhance the piano arrangements, regardless of how you choose to play them. Each track includes two measures of count-off clicks at the beginning. If the recording is too fast or too slow, use the online **PLAYBACK+** player to adjust it to a more comfortable tempo (speed).

Optional left-hand rhythm patterns are provided for when you are ready to move beyond the basic chords. The patterns are based on the three notes of the basic chords and appear as small, gray notes in the first line of each song. Feel free to use the suggested pattern throughout the song, or create your own. Sample rhythm patterns are shown below. (Of course, you can always play just the basic chords if you wish!)

Have fun! Whether you play with one hand or two, you'll sound great!

Sample Rhythm Patterns

4/4 Meter

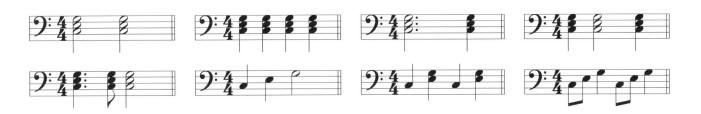

3/4 Meter

6/8 Meter

Also Available

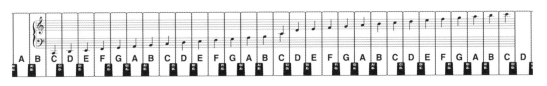

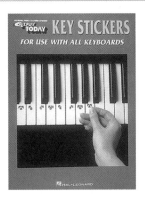

Hal Leonard Student Keyboard Guide HL00296039

Key Stickers HL00100016

Animal Crackers in My Soup

from CURLY TOP

Words by Ted Koehler
and Irving Caesar
Music by Ray Henderson

Moderately bright

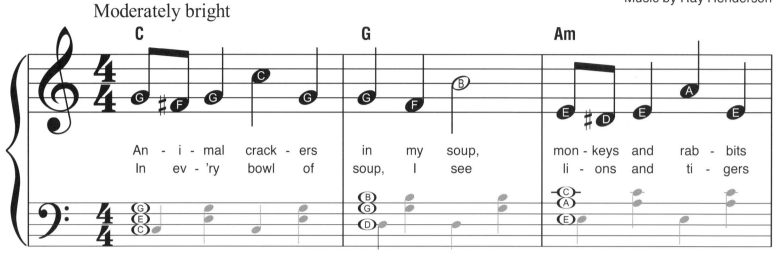

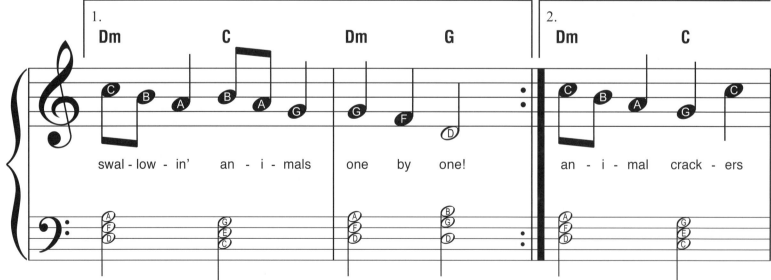

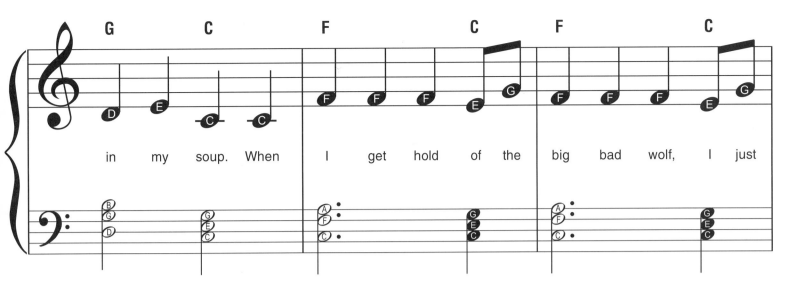

in my soup. When | I get hold of the | big bad wolf, I just

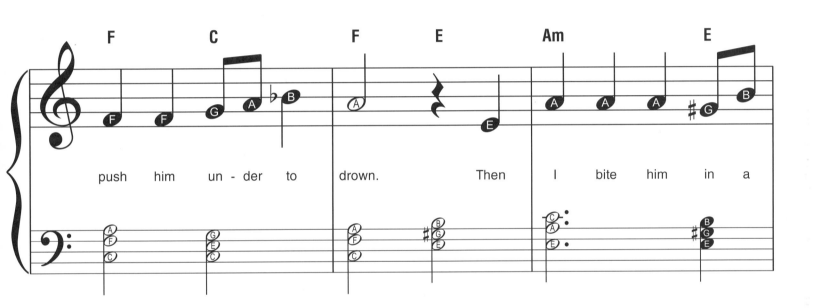

push him un - der to | drown. Then | I bite him in a

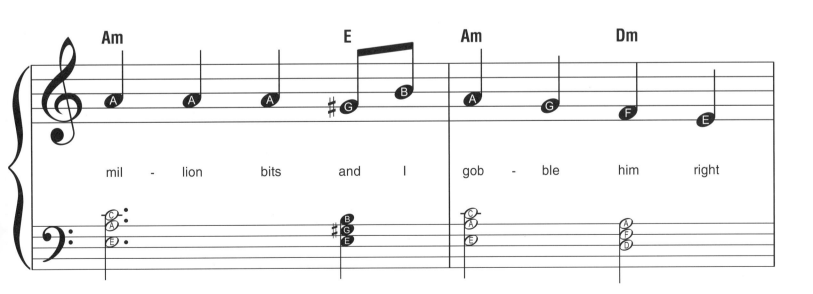

mil - lion bits and I | gob - ble him right

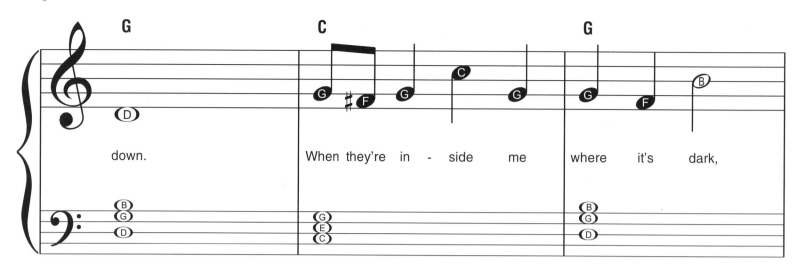

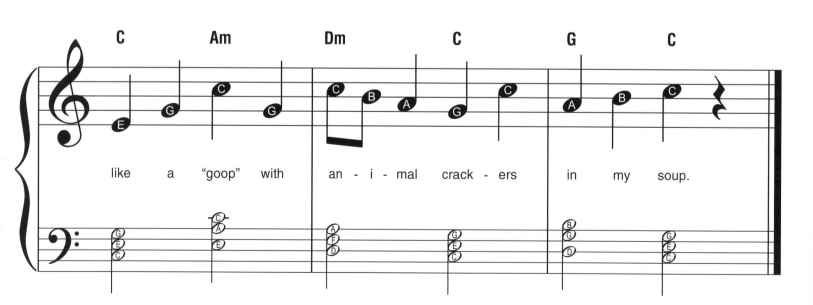

Castle on a Cloud
from LES MISÉRABLES

Music by Claude-Michel Schönberg
Lyrics by Alain Boublil,
Jean-Marc Natel and Herbert Kretzmer

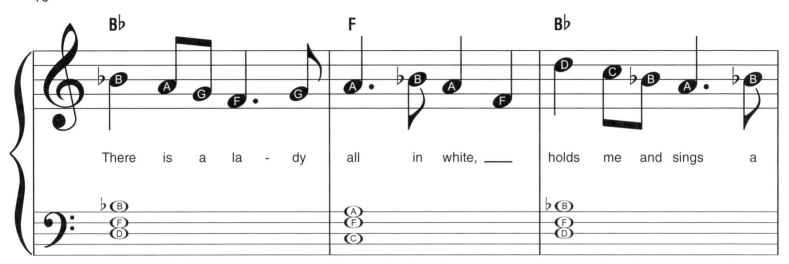

There is a la - dy all in white, ___ holds me and sings a

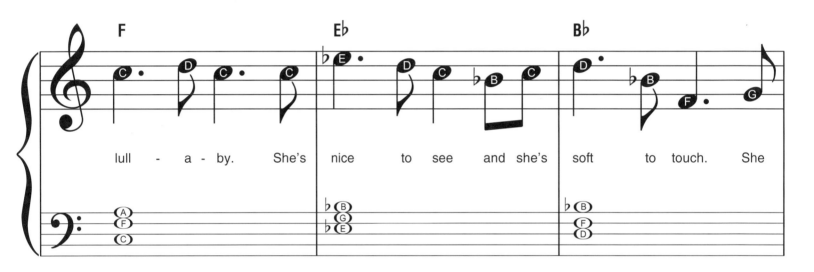

lull - a - by. She's nice to see and she's soft to touch. She

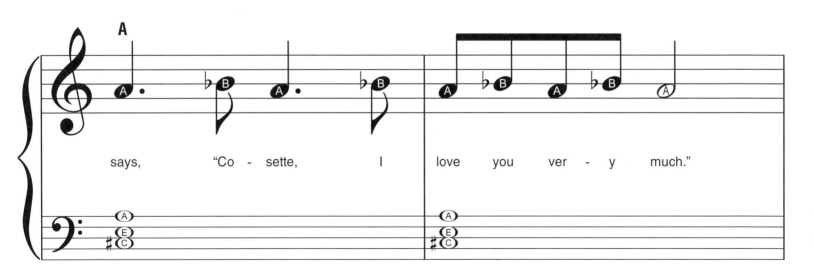

says, "Co - sette, I love you ver - y much."

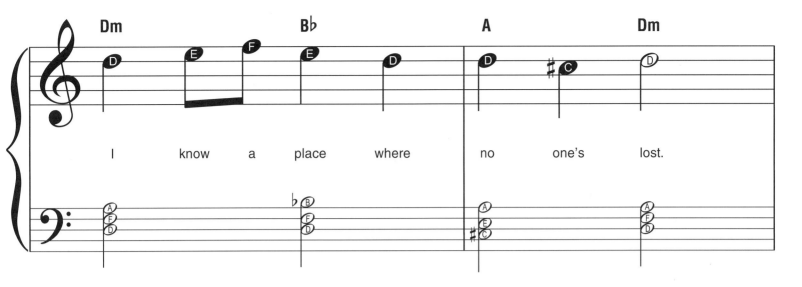

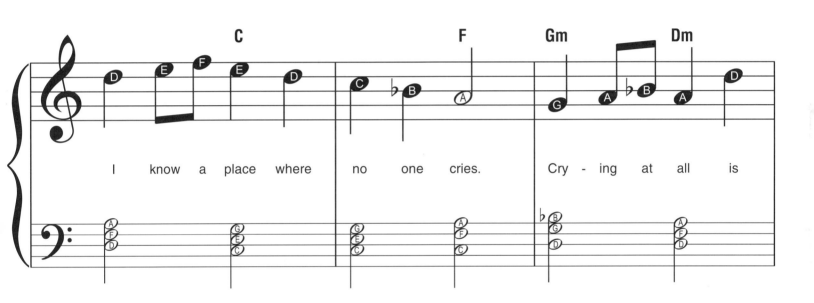

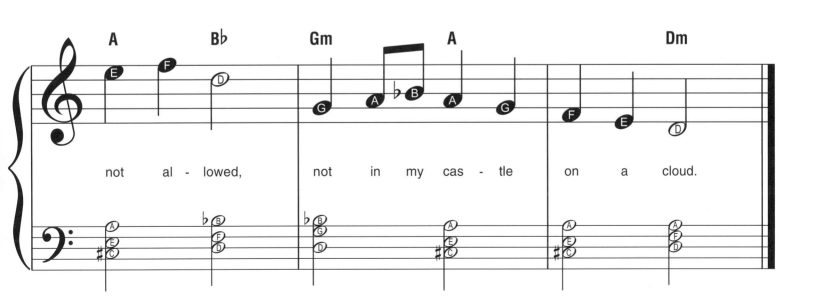

"C" Is for Cookie

from the Television Series SESAME STREET

Words and Music by
Joe Raposo

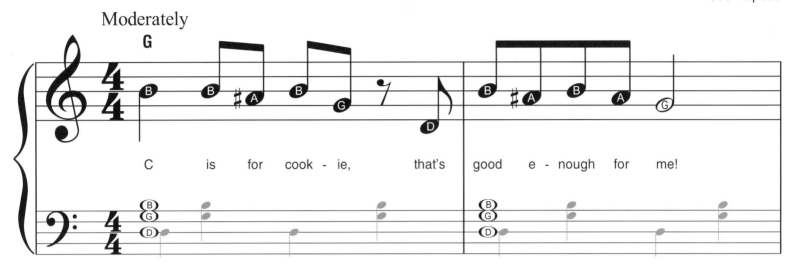

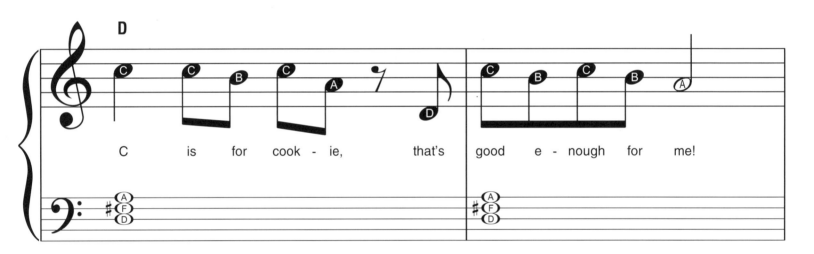

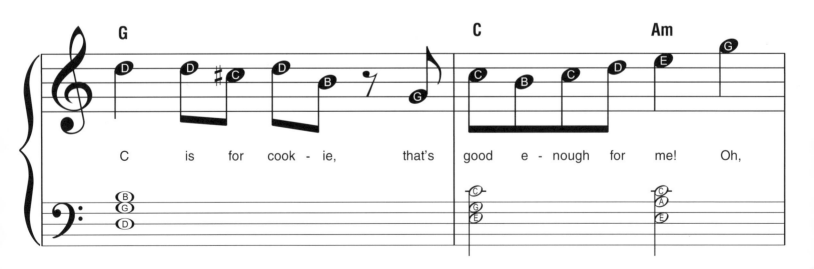

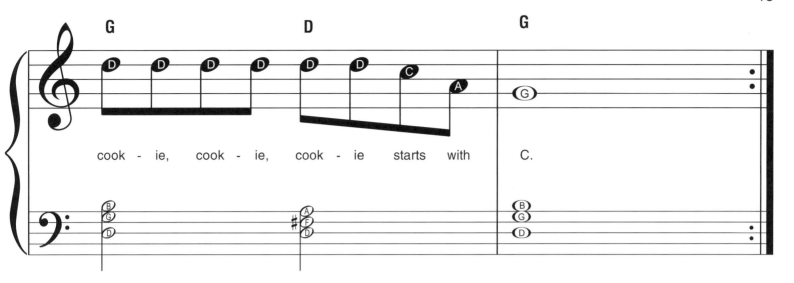

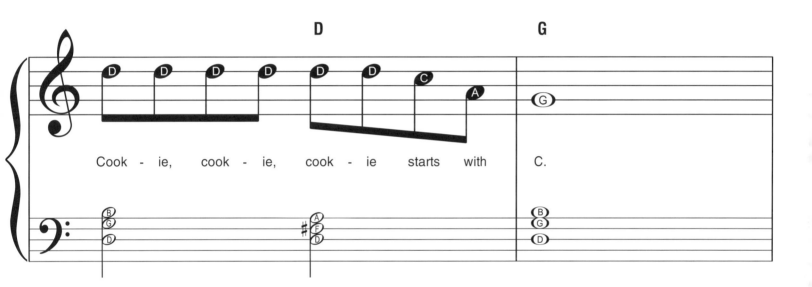

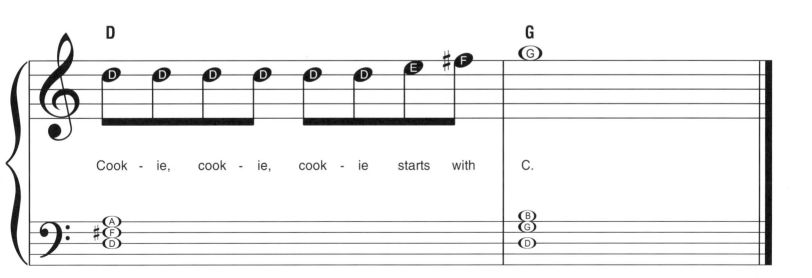

The Candy Man
from WILLY WONKA AND THE CHOCOLATE FACTORY

Words and Music by Leslie Bricusse
and Anthony Newley

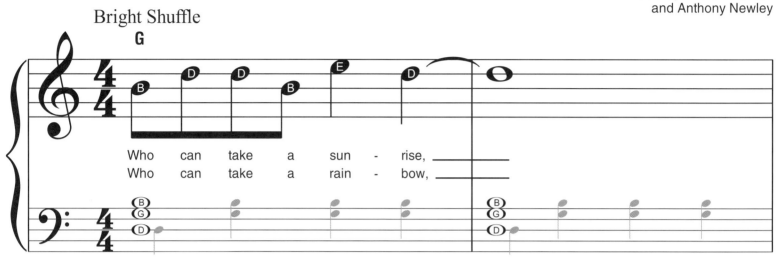

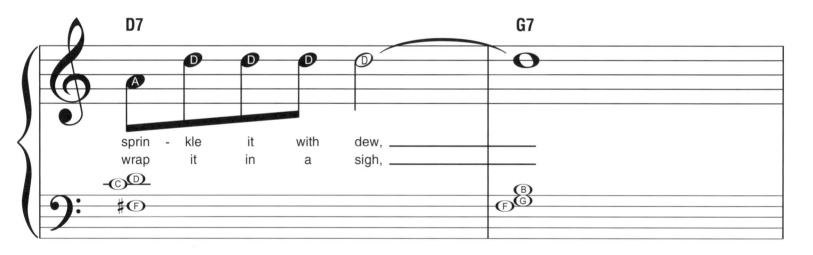

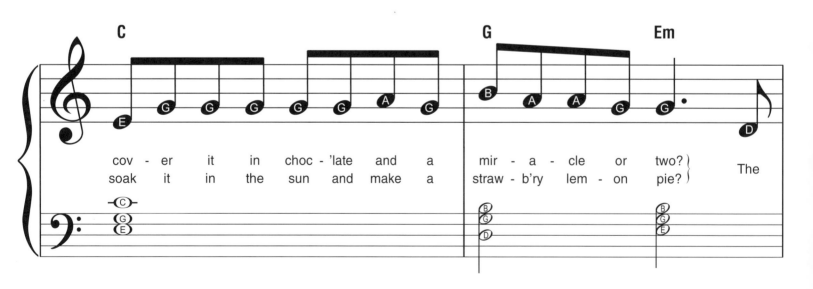

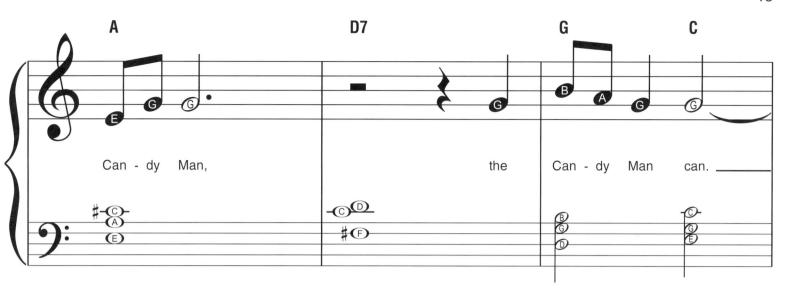

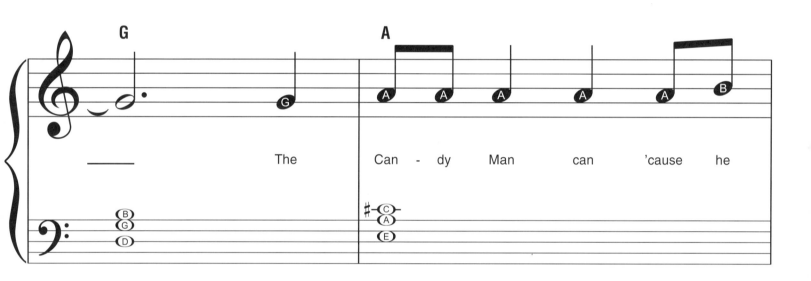

Do-Re-Mi

from THE SOUND OF MUSIC

Lyrics by Oscar Hammerstein II
Music by Richard Rodgers

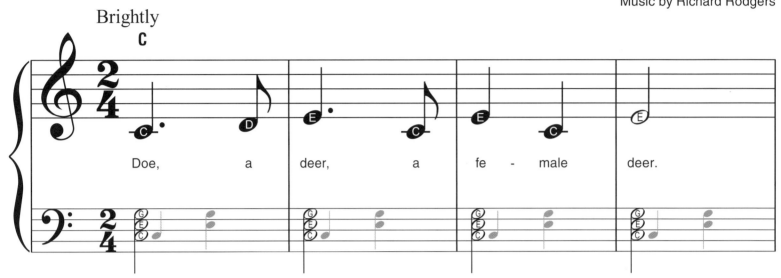

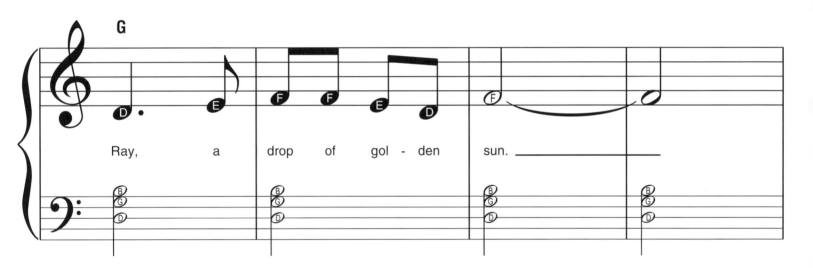

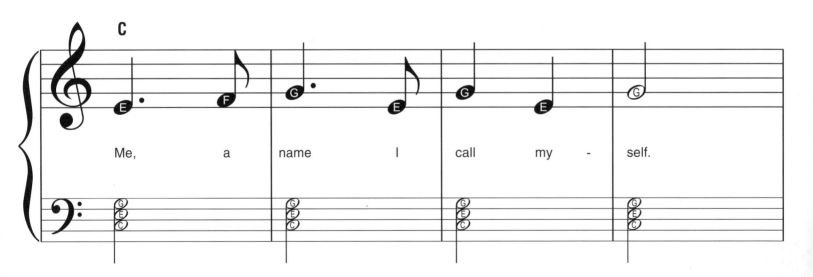

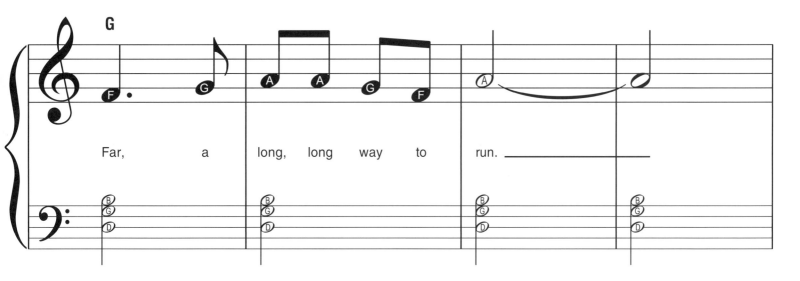

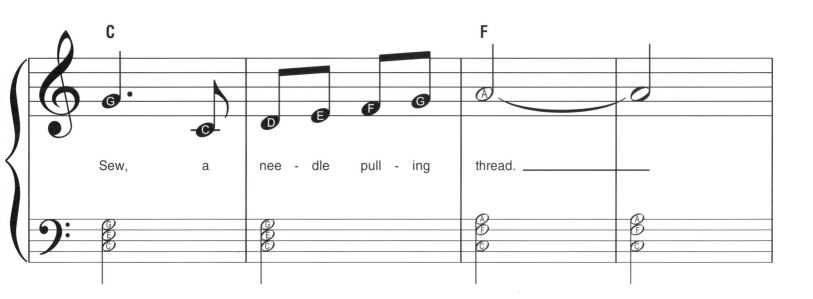

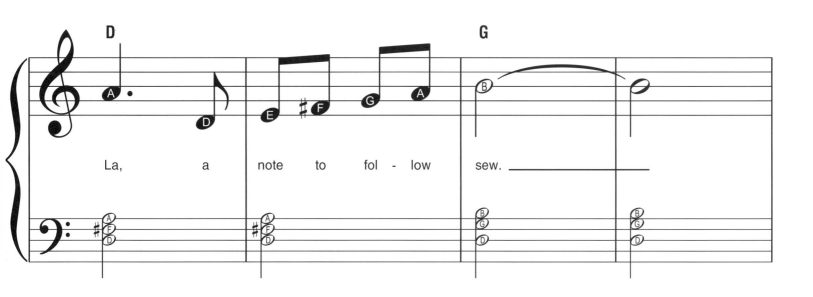

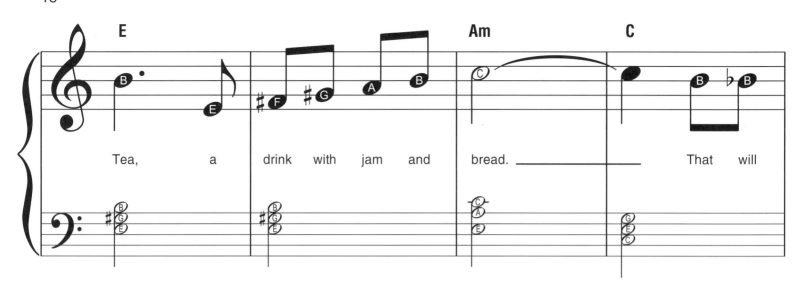

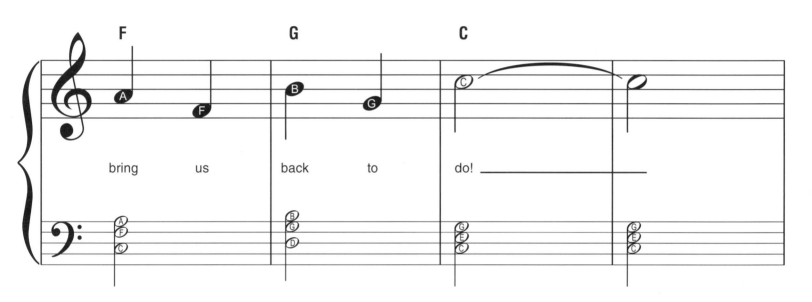

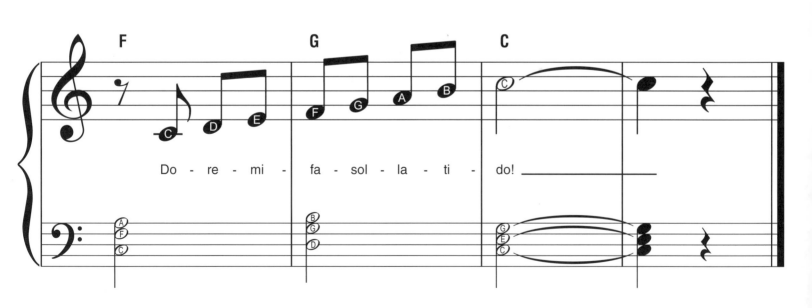

Hakuna Matata
from THE LION KING

Music by Elton John
Lyrics by Tim Rice

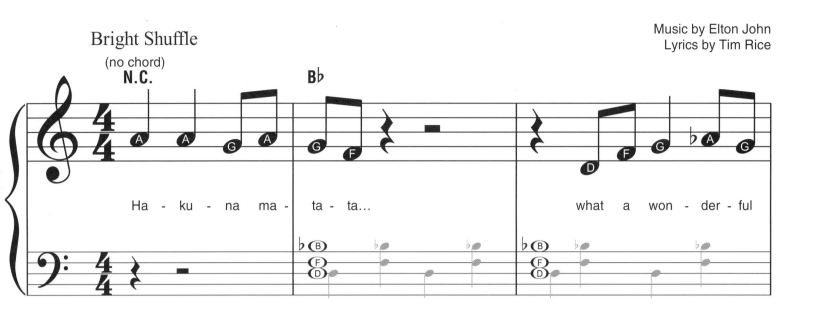

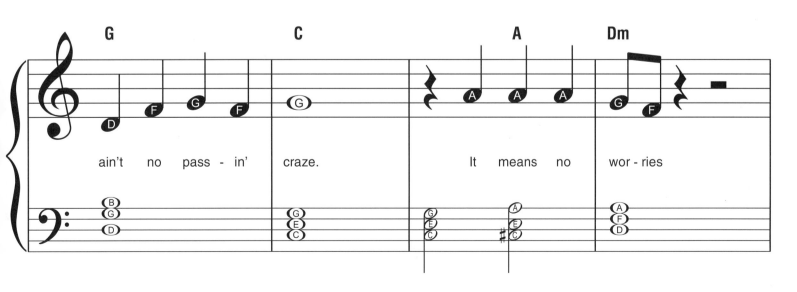

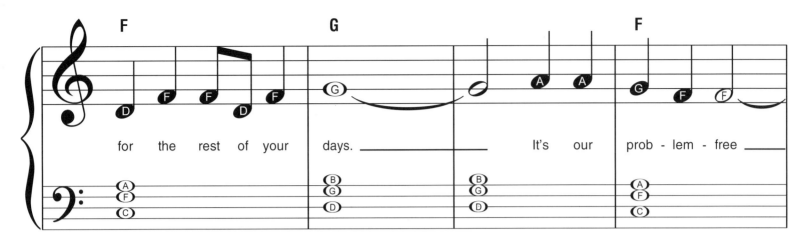

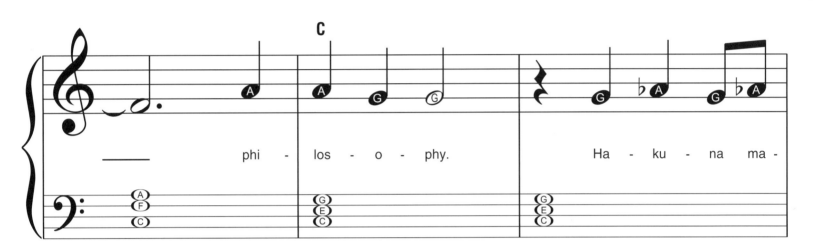

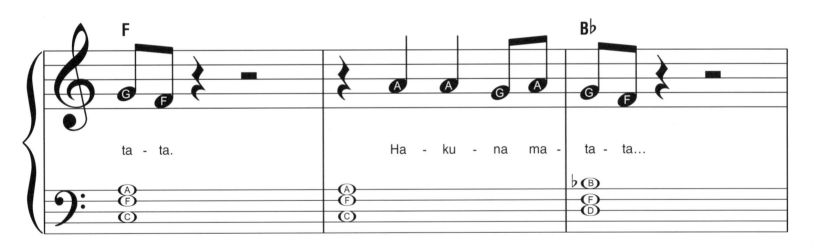

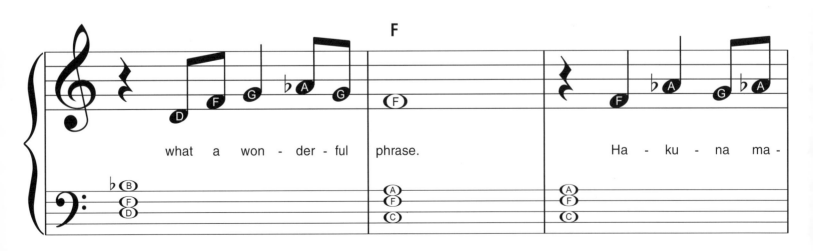

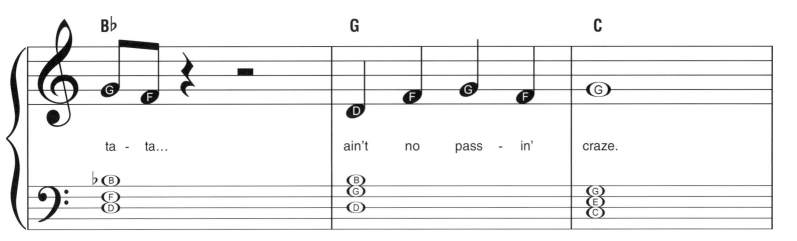

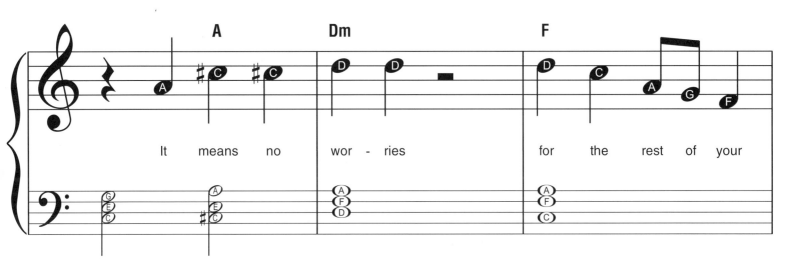

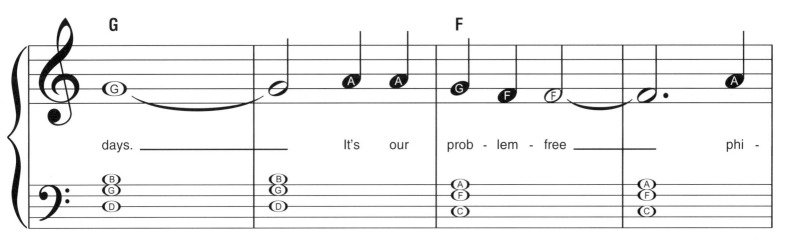

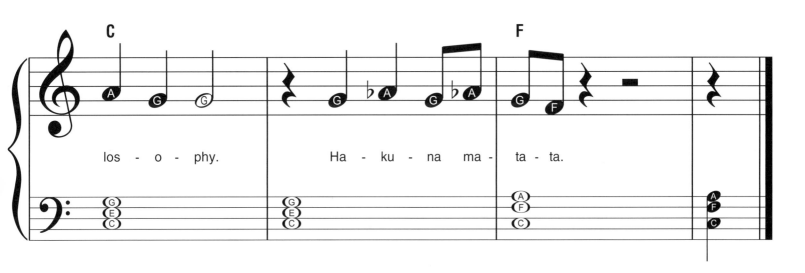

Happy Birthday to You

Words and Music by Mildred J. Hill
and Patty S. Hill

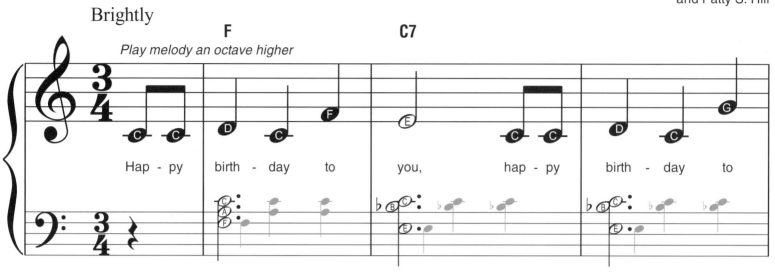

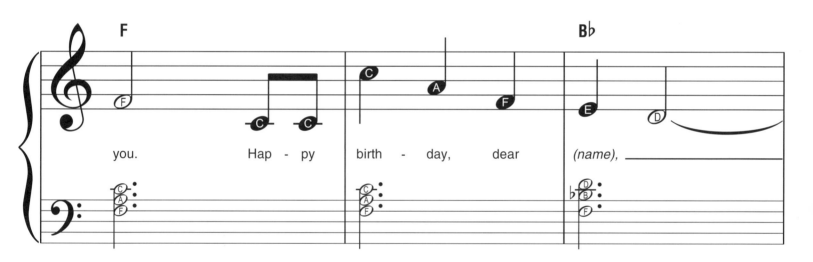

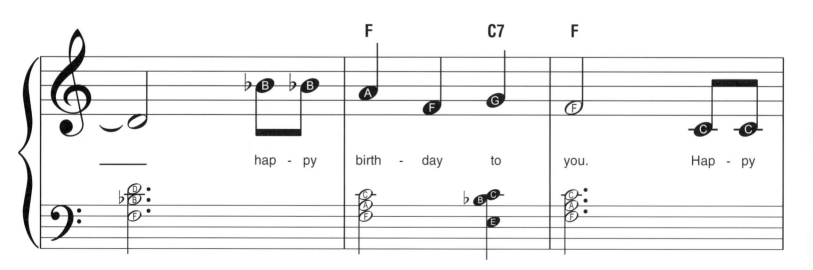

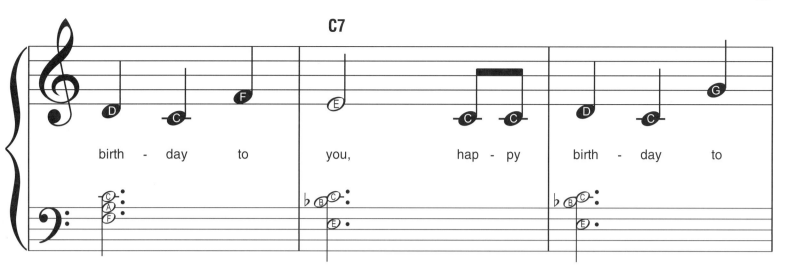

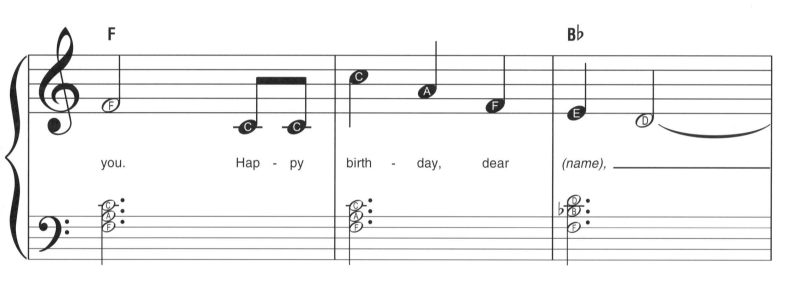

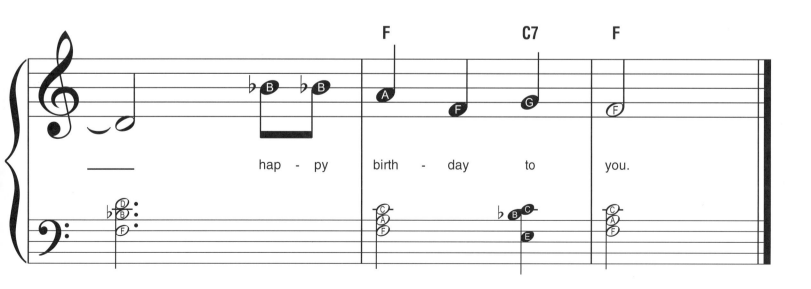

The Hokey Pokey

Words and Music by Charles P. Macak,
Tafft Baker and Larry LaPrise

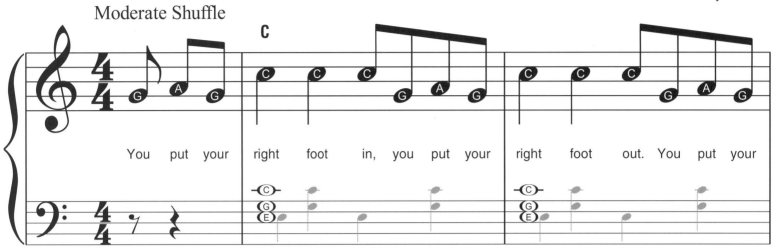

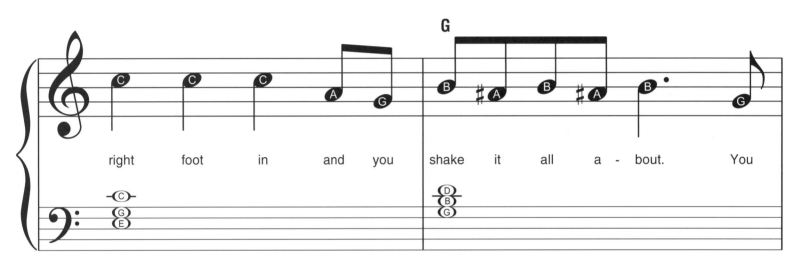

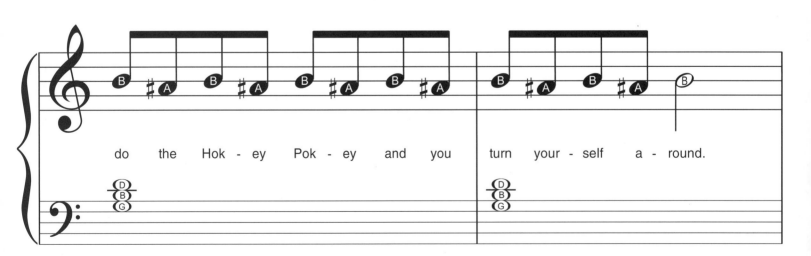

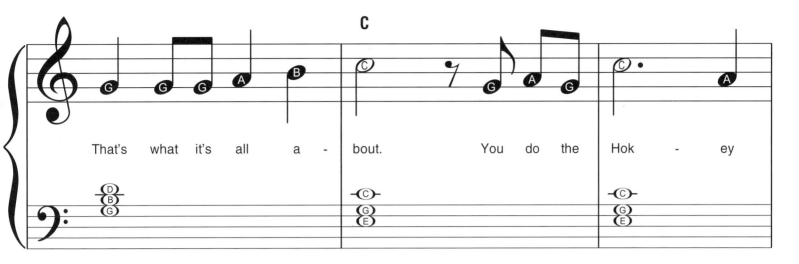

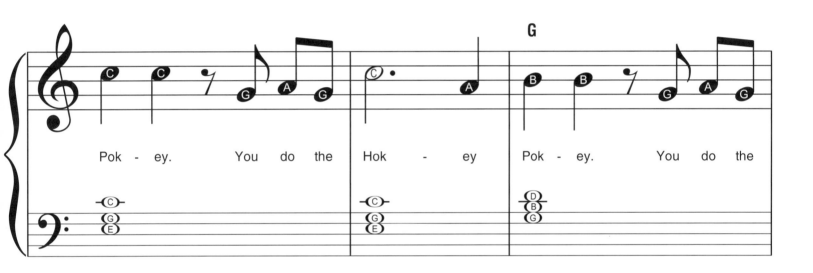

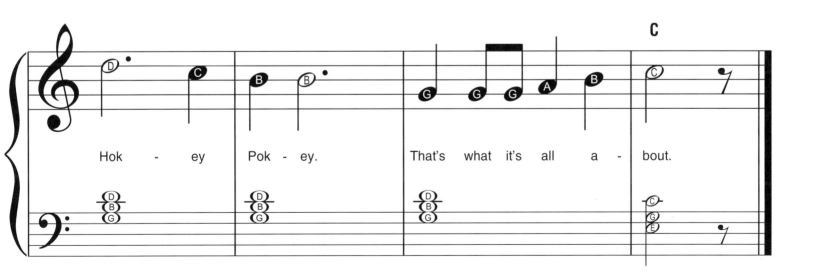

Hot Dog!
from MICKEY MOUSE CLUBHOUSE

Words and Music by John Flansburgh
and John Linnell

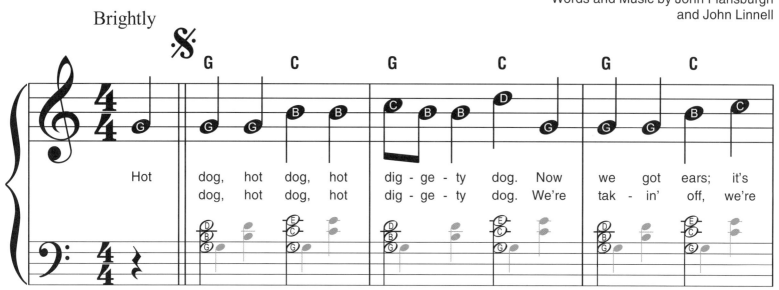

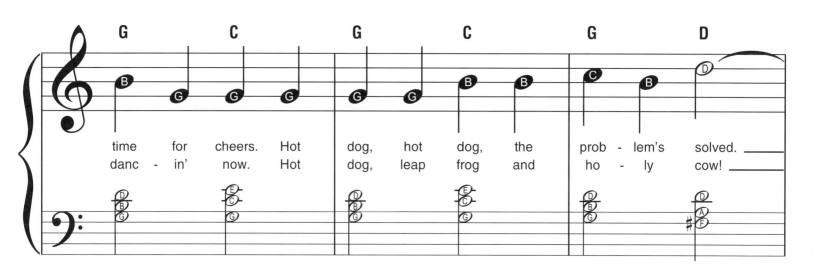

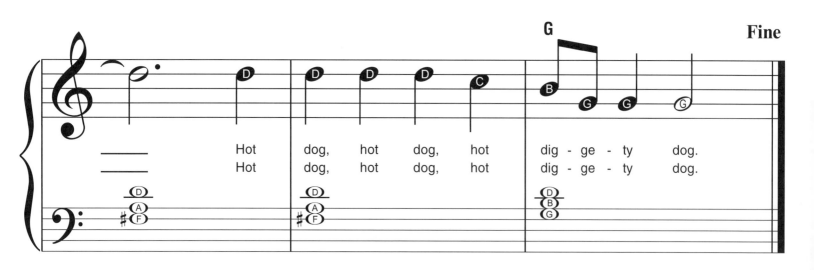

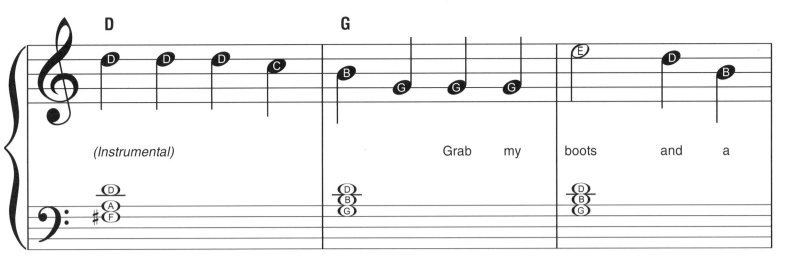

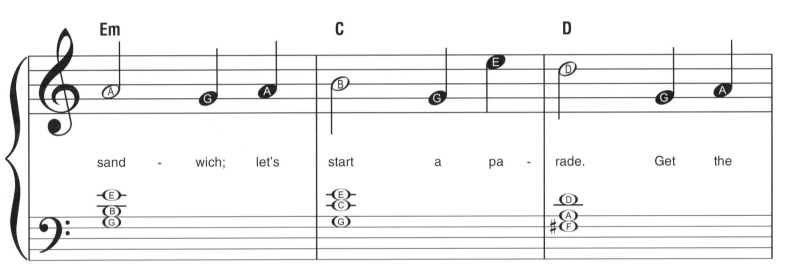

D.S. al Fine
(Return to 𝄋
and play to Fine)

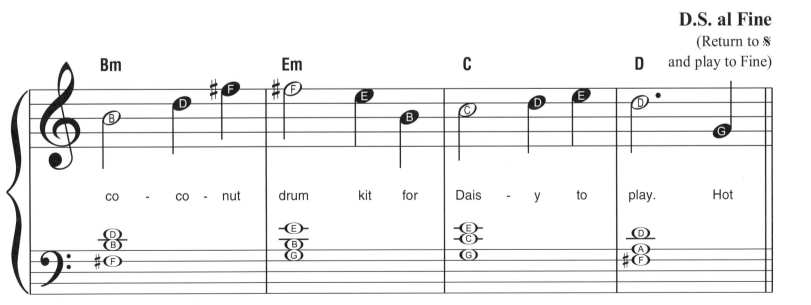

How Much Is That Doggie in the Window

Words and Music by
Bob Merrill

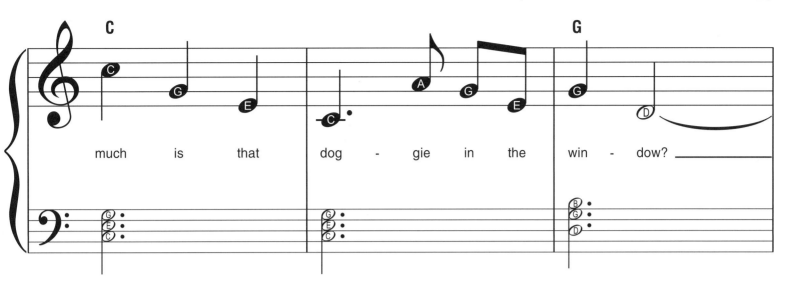

much is that dog - gie in the win - dow? _____

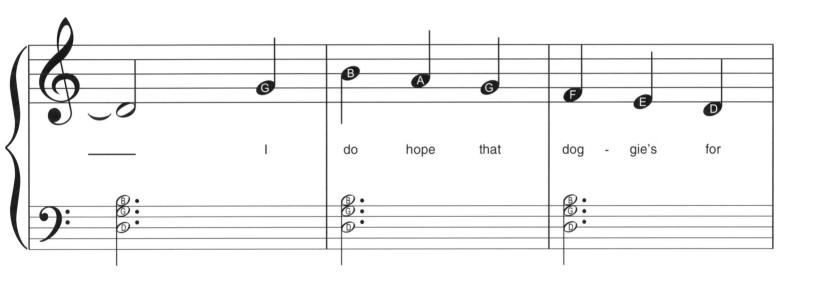

_____ I do hope that dog - gie's for

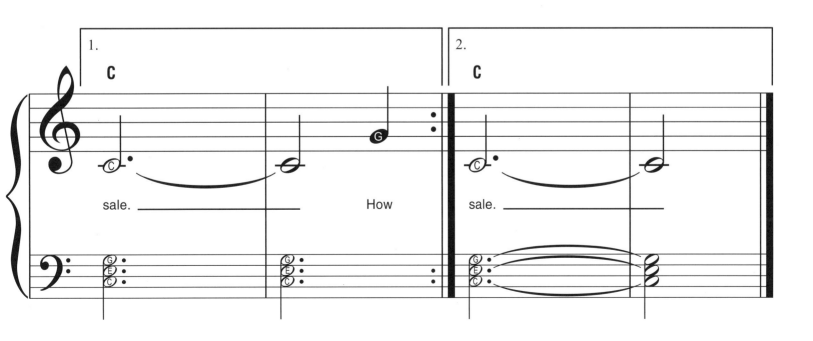

sale. _____ How

sale. _____

Hush, Little Baby

Carolina Folk Lullaby

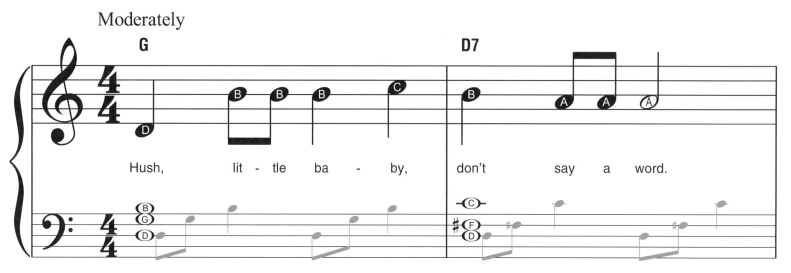

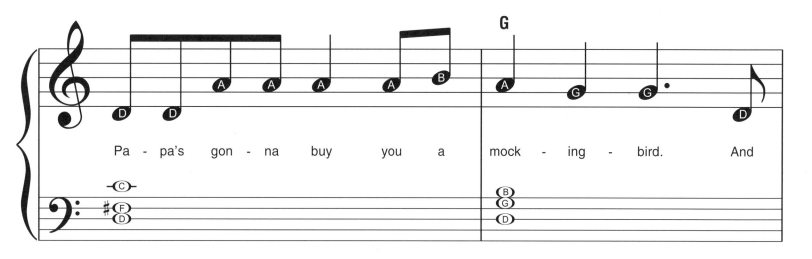

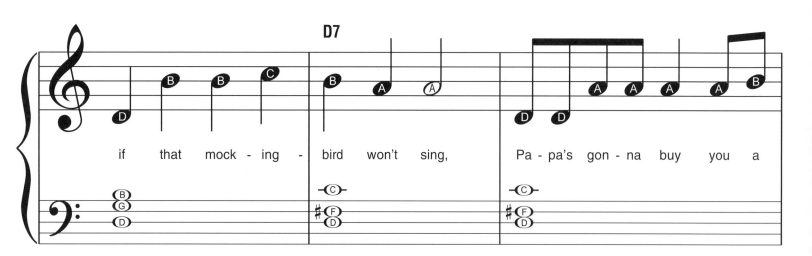

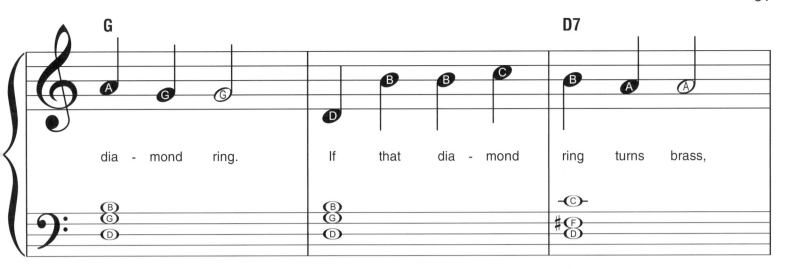

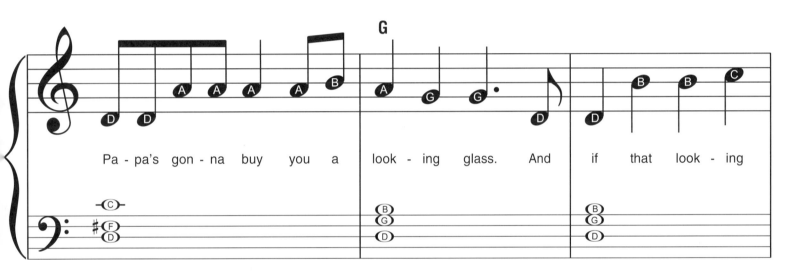

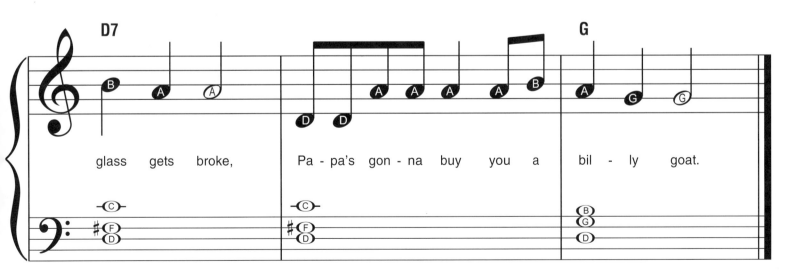

It's a Small World

from Disney Parks' "it's a small world" attraction

Words and Music by Richard M. Sherman
and Robert B. Sherman

Brightly

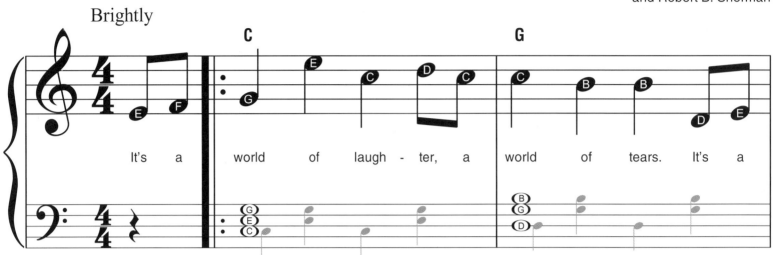

It's a world of laugh - ter, a world of tears. It's a

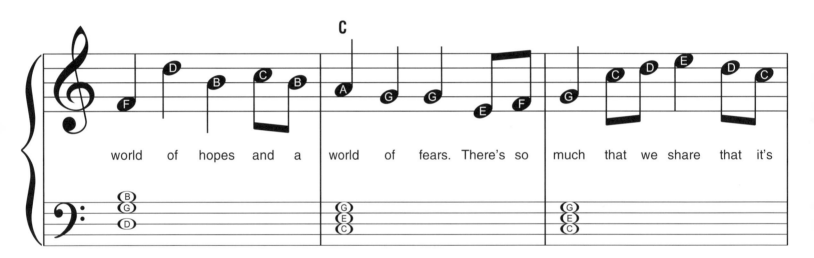

world of hopes and a world of fears. There's so much that we share that it's

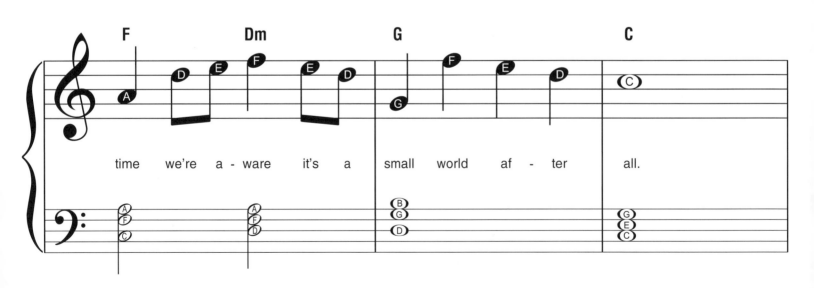

time we're a - ware it's a small world af - ter all.

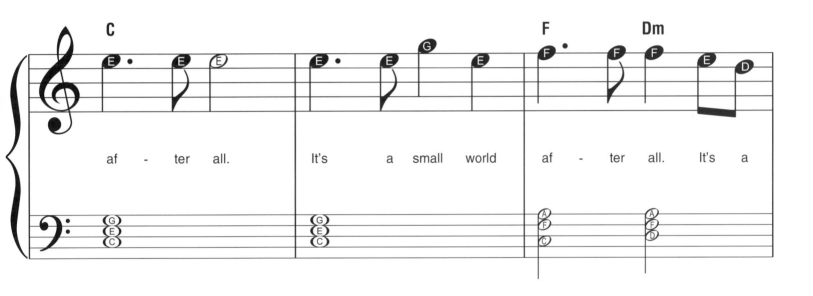

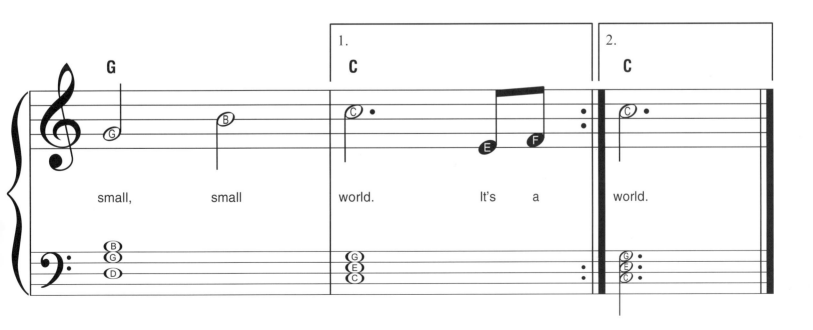

Mickey Mouse March
from THE MICKEY MOUSE CLUB

Words and Music by
Jimmie Dodd

Bright March

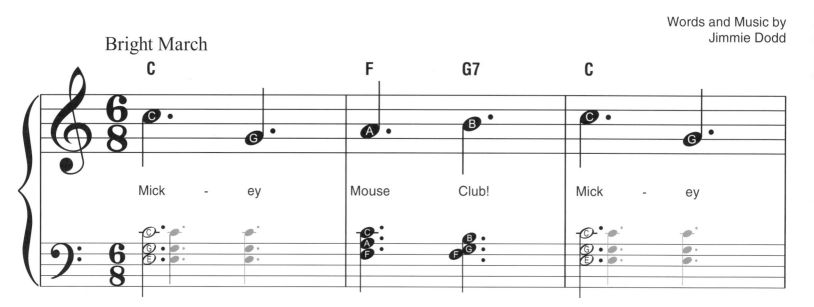

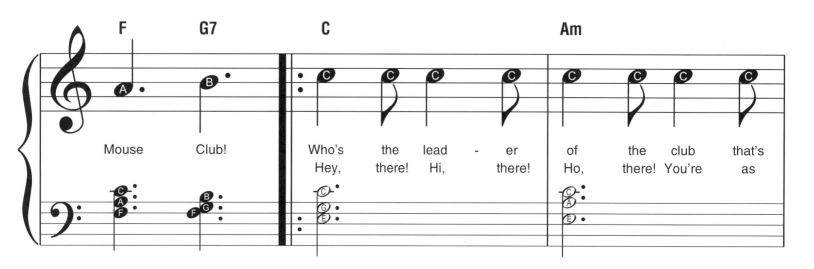

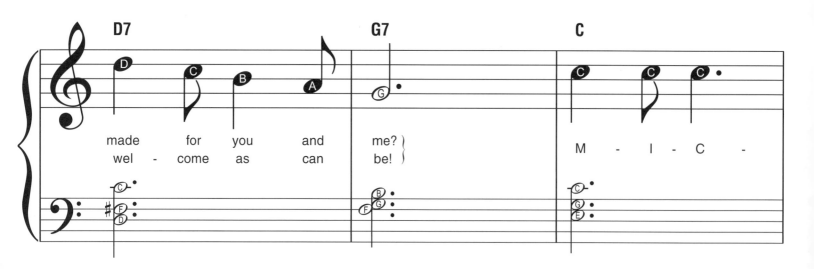

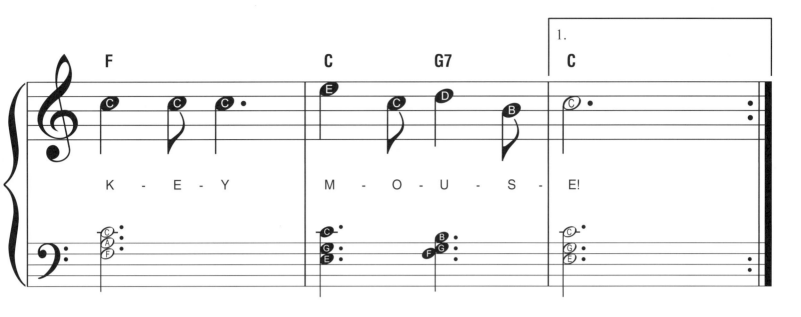

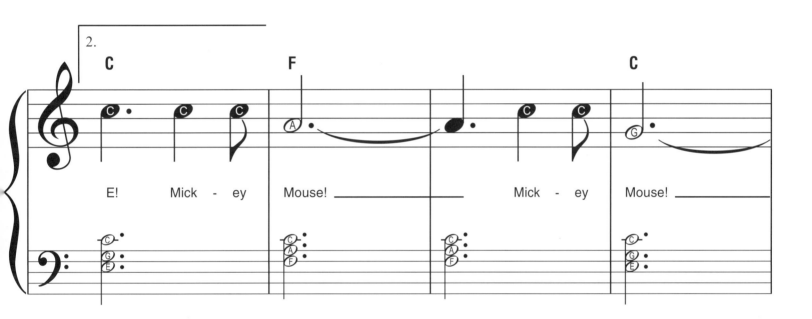

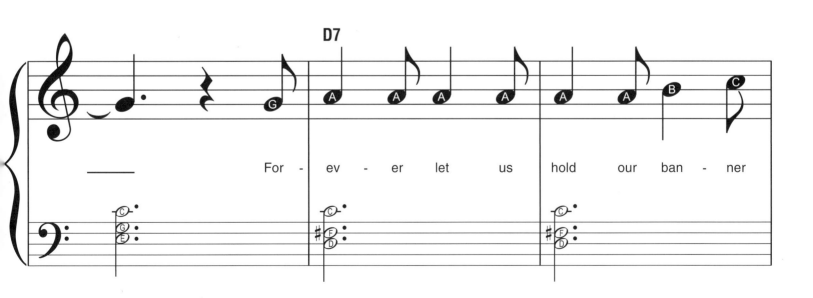

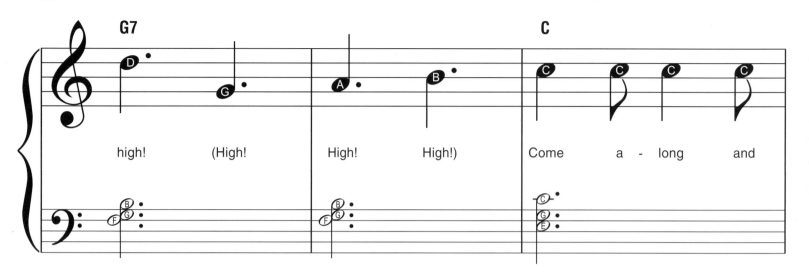

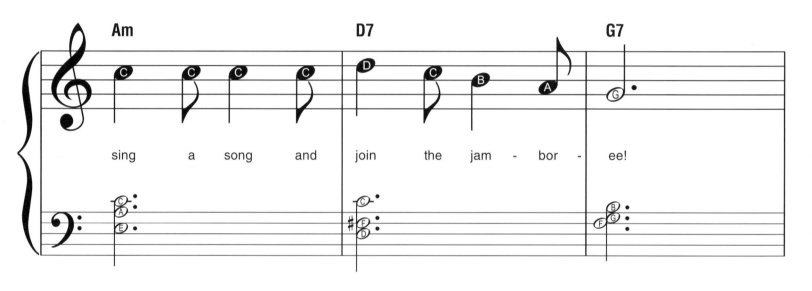

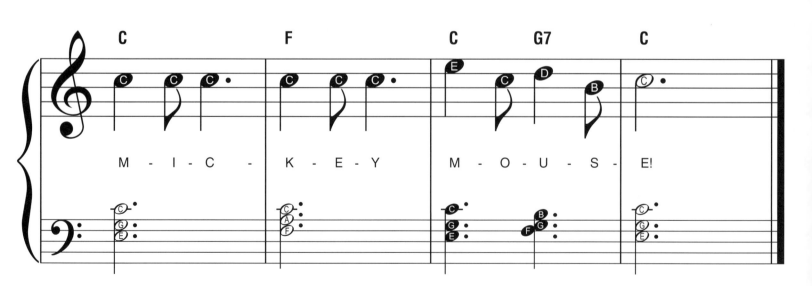

I Whistle a Happy Tune

from THE KING AND I

Lyrics by Oscar Hammerstein II
Music by Richard Rodgers

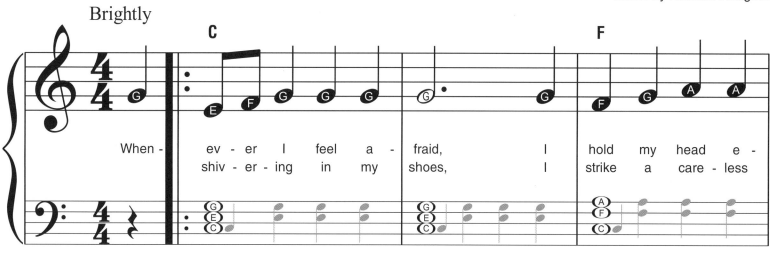

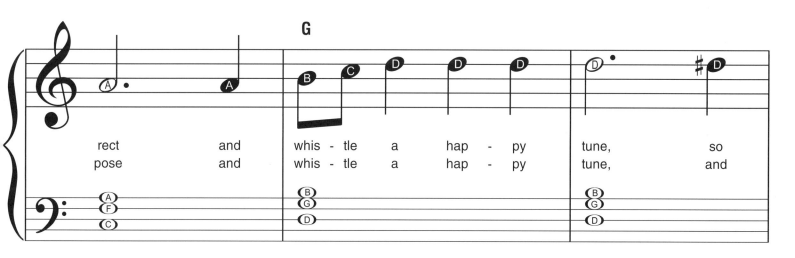

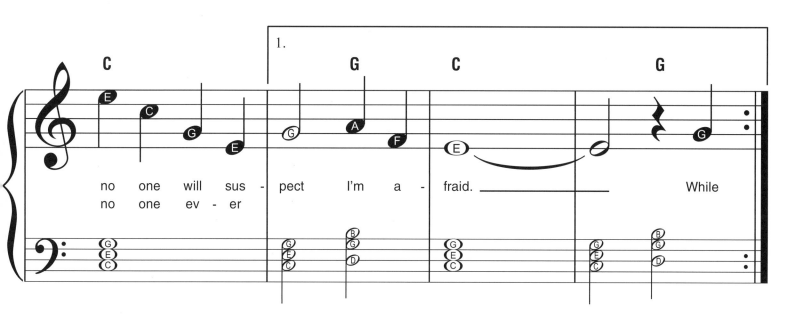

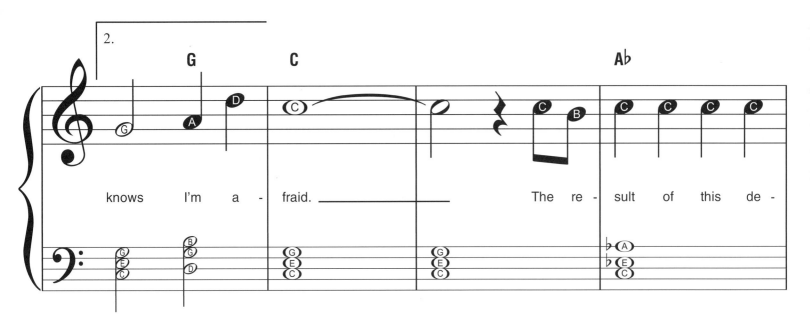

knows I'm a - fraid. _____ The re - sult of this de -

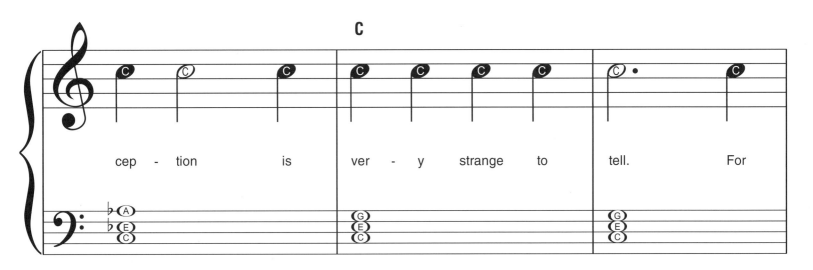

cep - tion is ver - y strange to tell. For

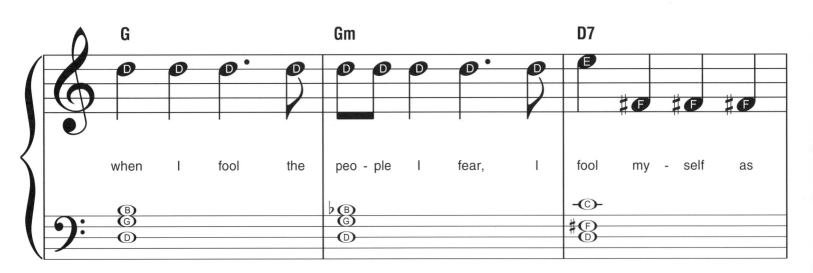

when I fool the peo - ple I fear, I fool my - self as

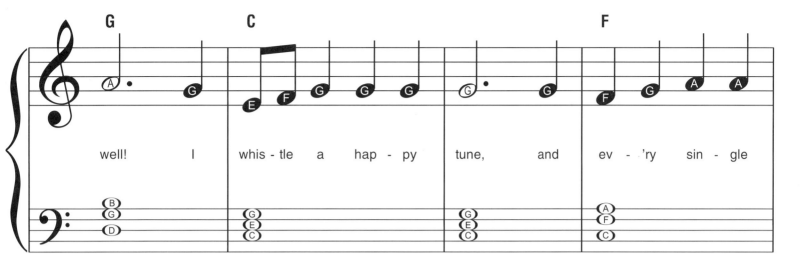

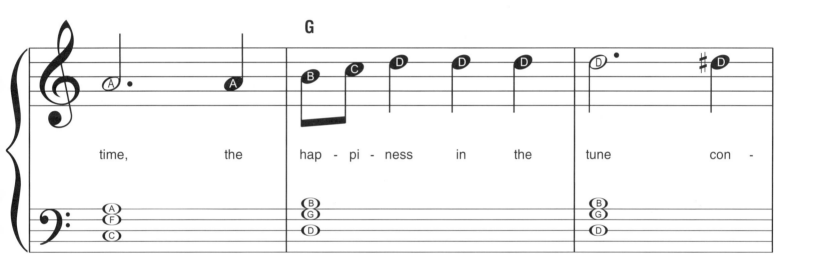

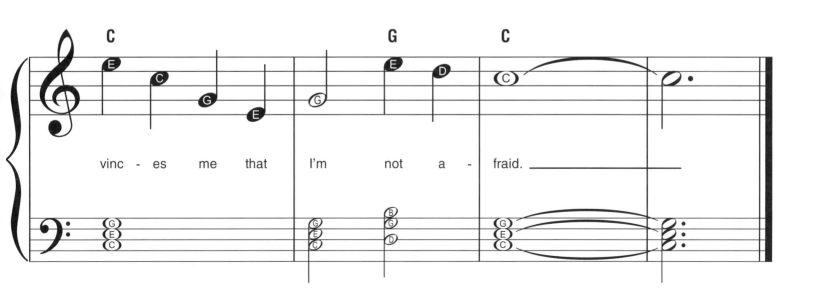

Old MacDonald

Traditional Children's Song

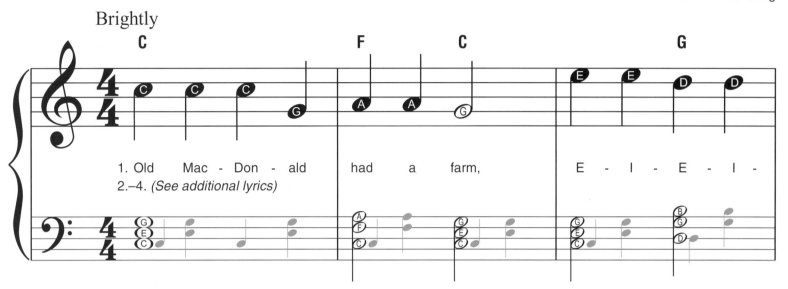

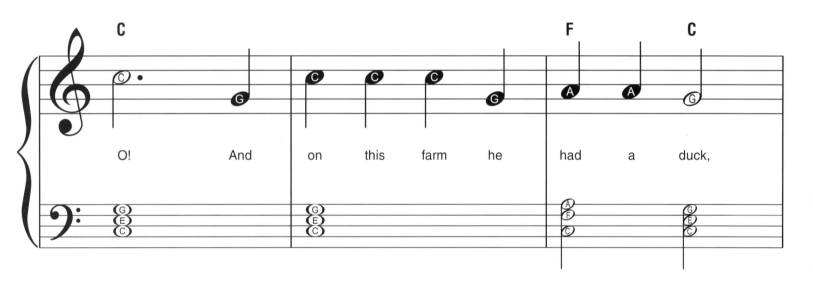

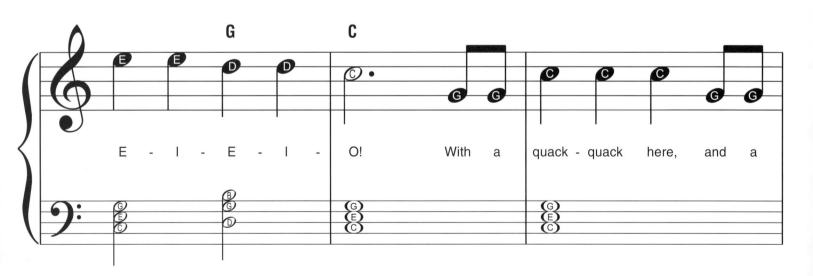

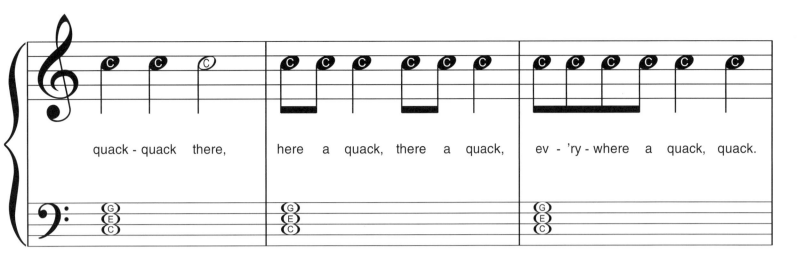

quack - quack there,   here a quack, there a quack,   ev - 'ry - where a quack, quack.

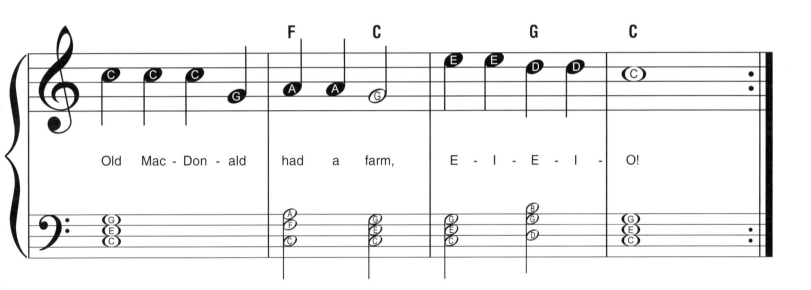

Old   Mac - Don - ald   had   a   farm,   E - I - E - I -   O!

Additional Lyrics

2. Old MacDonald had a farm,
   E-I-E-I-O!
   And on his farm he had a chick,
   E-I-E-I-O!
   With a chick, chick here,
   And a chick, chick there,
   Here a chick, there a chick,
   Everywhere a chick, chick.
   Old MacDonald had a farm,
   E-I-E-I-O!

3. Cow – moo, moo
4. Pig – oink, oink

Peter Cottontail

Words and Music by Steve Nelson
and Jack Rollins

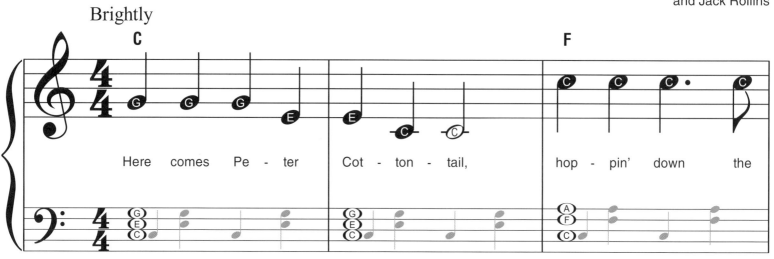

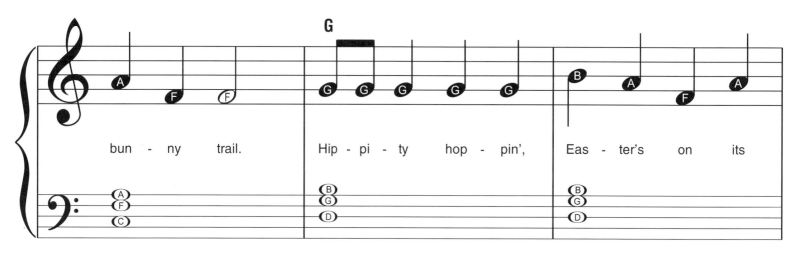

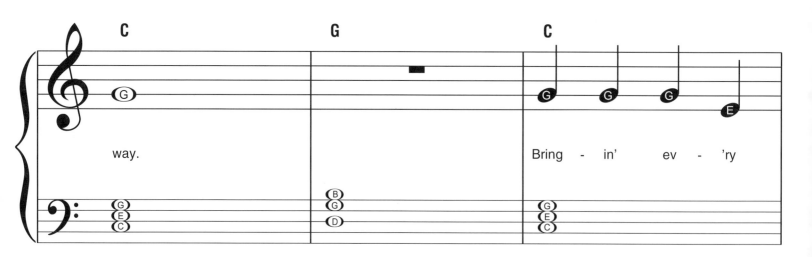

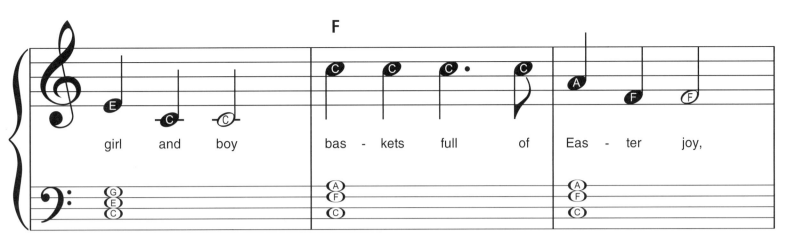

girl and boy bas- kets full of Eas - ter joy,

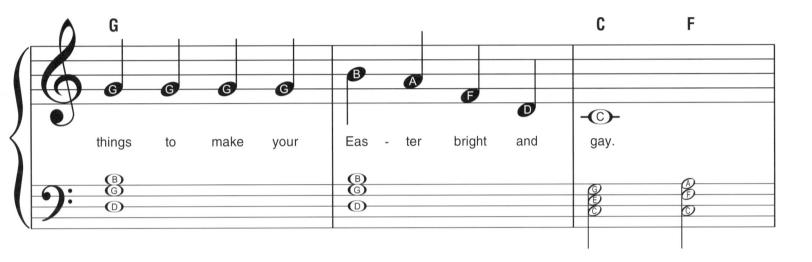

things to make your Eas - ter bright and gay.

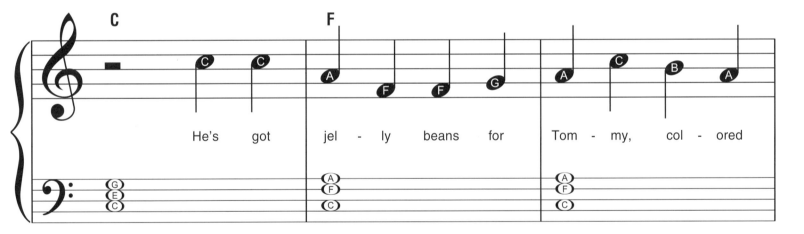

He's got jel - ly beans for Tom - my, col - ored

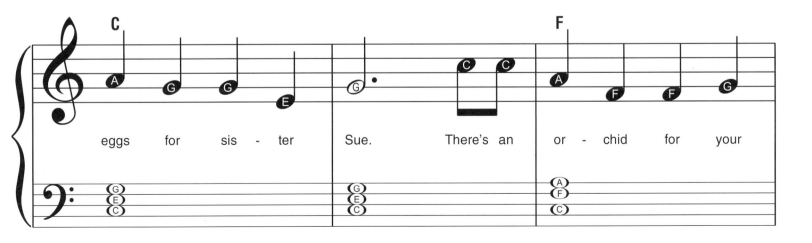

eggs for sis - ter Sue. There's an or - chid for your

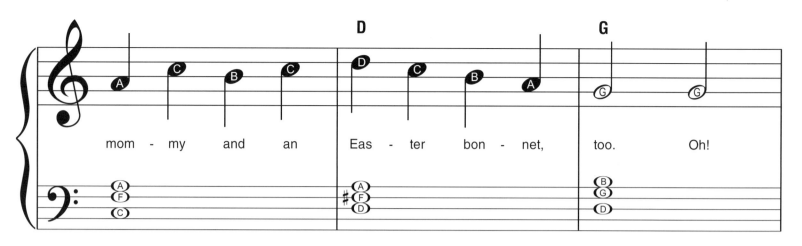

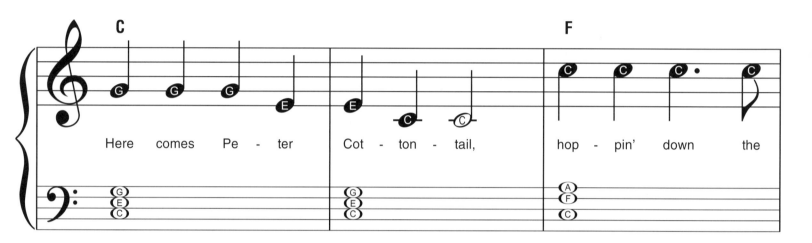

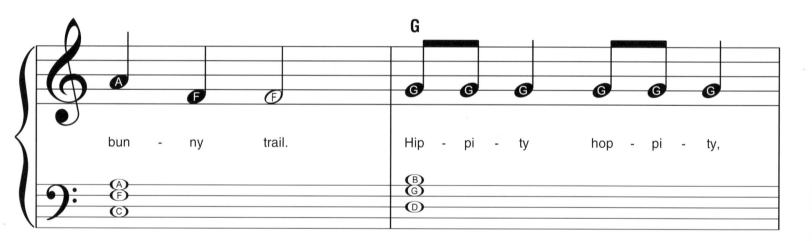

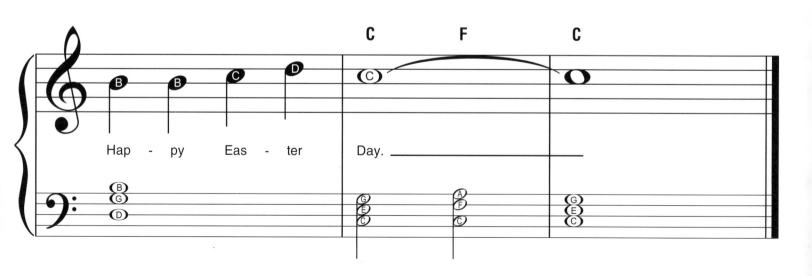

On Top of Spaghetti

Words and Music by
Tom Glazer

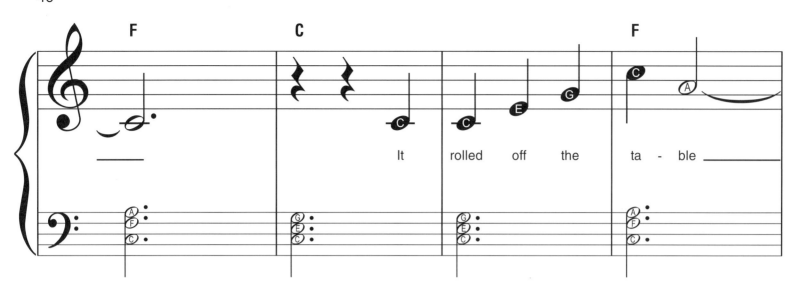

It rolled off the ta - ble

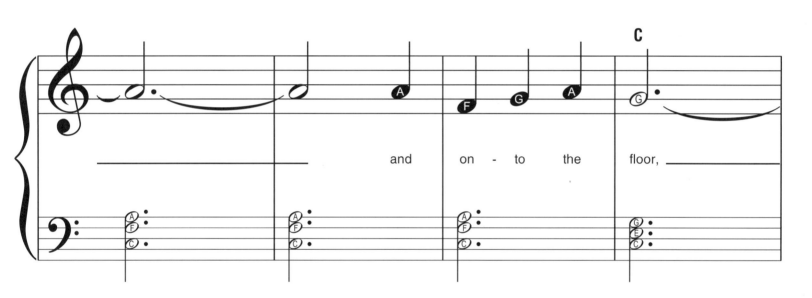

and on - to the floor,

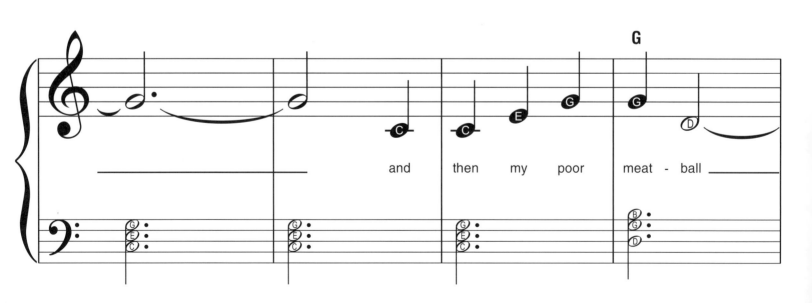

and then my poor meat - ball

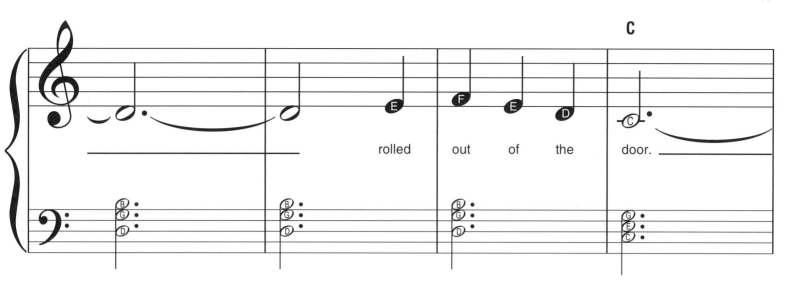

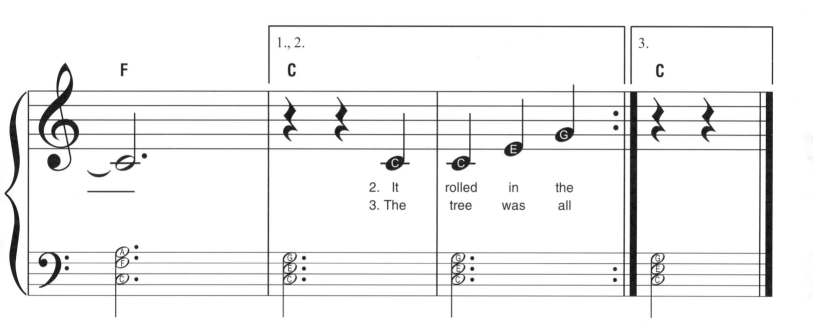

Additional Lyrics

2. It rolled in the garden and under a bush,
   And then my poor meatball was nothing but mush.
   The mush was as tasty as tasty could be,
   And early next summer, it grew into a tree.

3. The tree was all covered with beautiful moss.
   It grew lovely meatballs and tomato sauce.
   So if you eat spaghetti all covered with cheese,
   Hold on to your meatballs and don't ever sneeze!

Puff the Magic Dragon

Words and Music by Lenny Lipton
and Peter Yarrow

Moderately

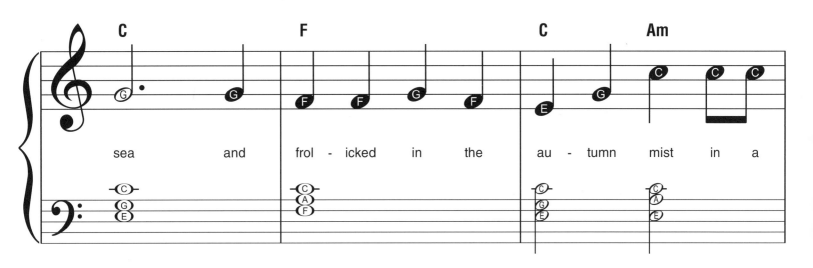

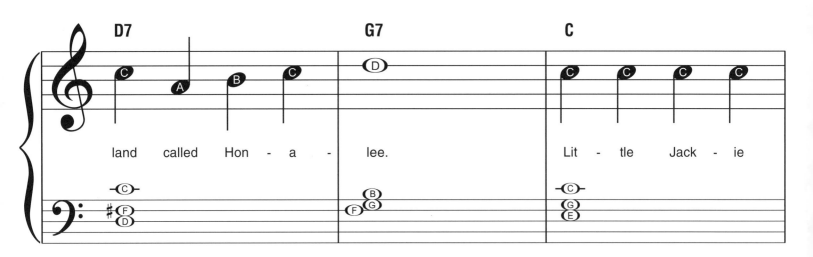

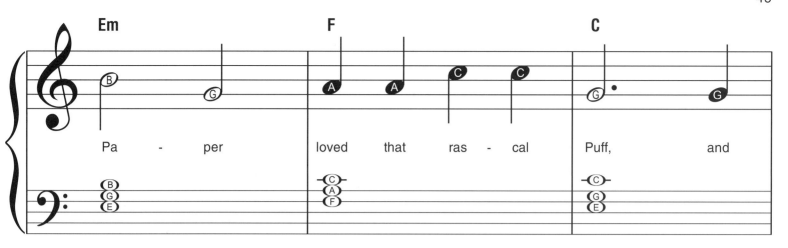

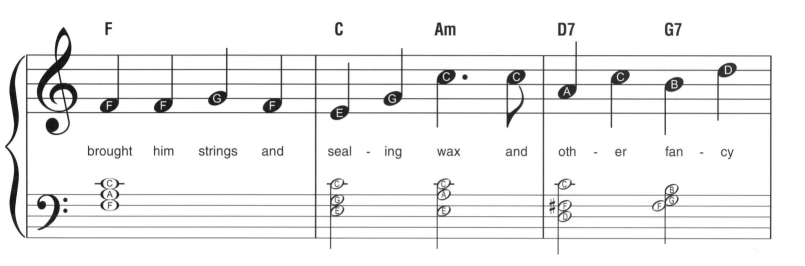

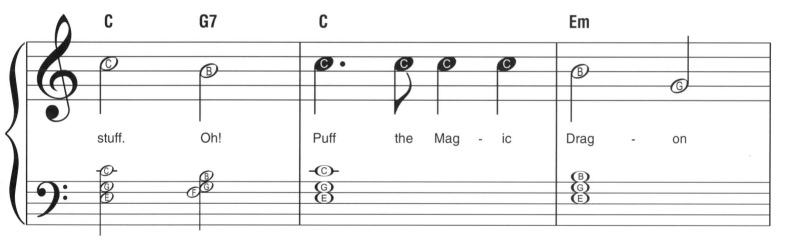

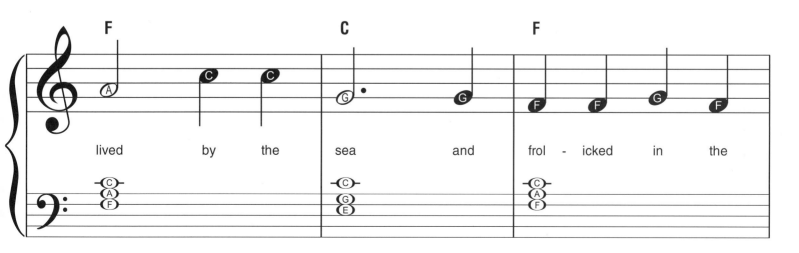

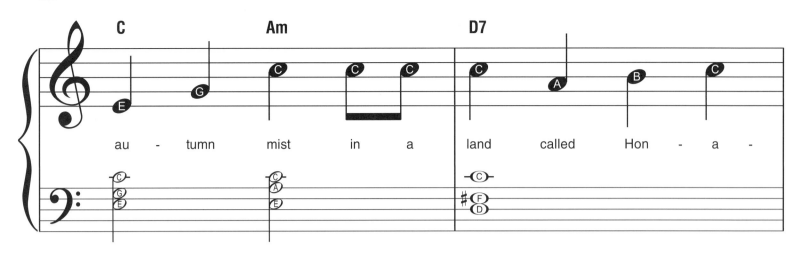

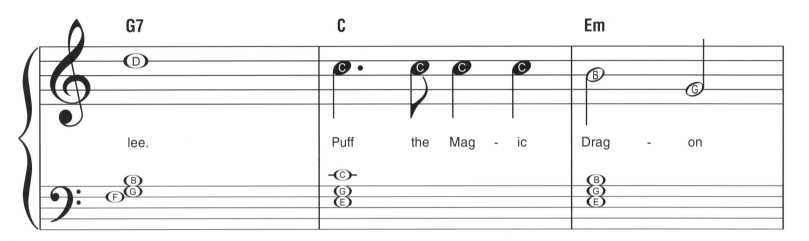

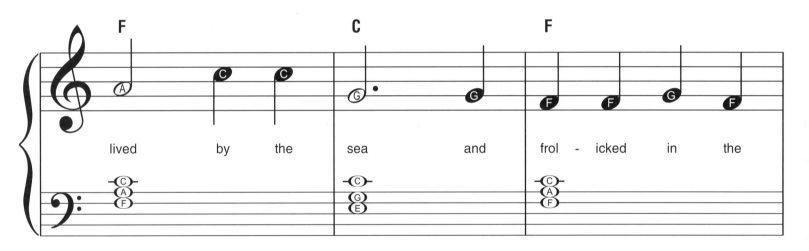

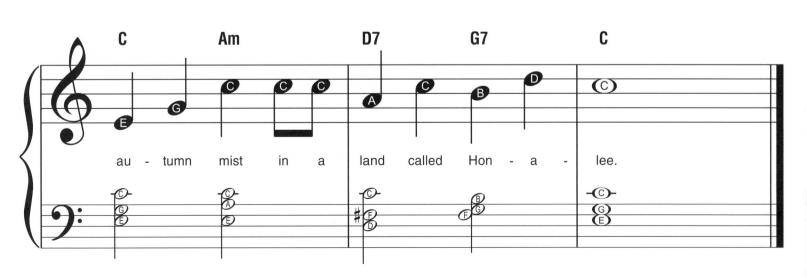

Rubber Duckie
from the Television Series SESAME STREET

Words and Music by
Jeff Moss

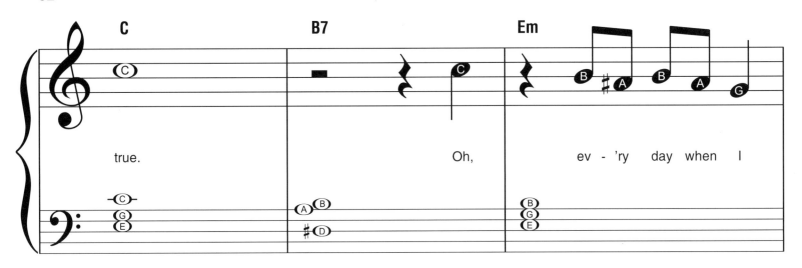

C   B7   Em

true.   Oh,   ev - 'ry   day   when   I

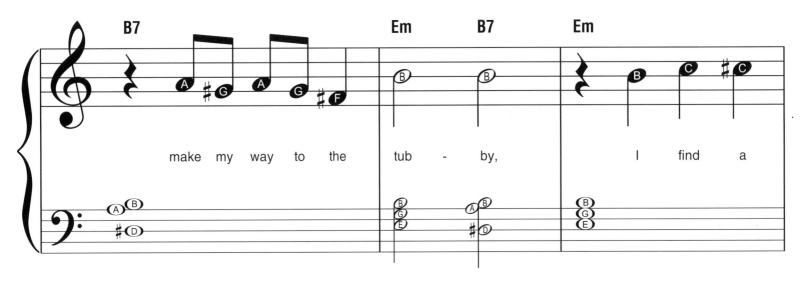

B7   Em   B7   Em

make my way to the   tub - by,   I   find   a

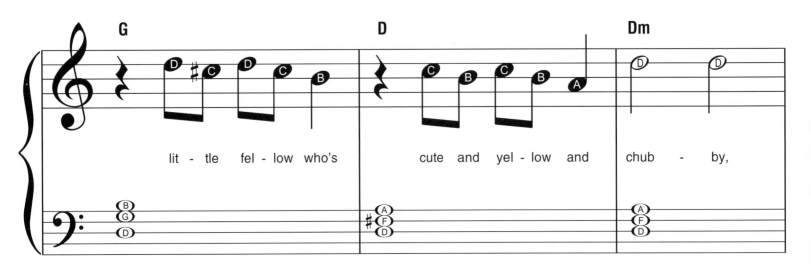

G   D   Dm

lit - tle fel - low who's   cute and yel - low and   chub - by,

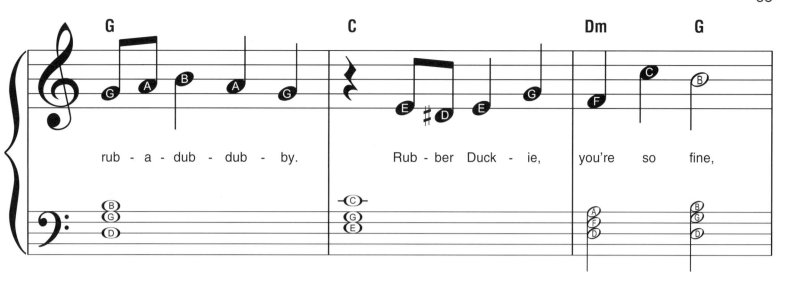

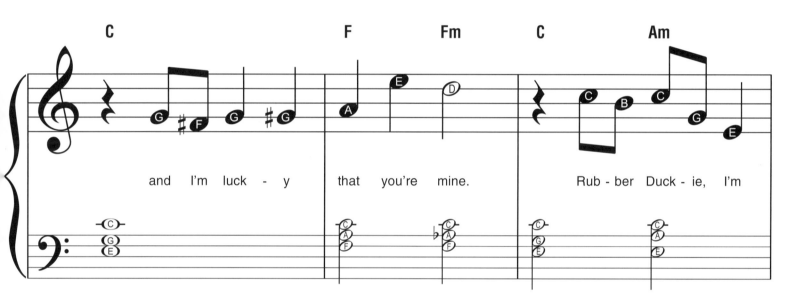

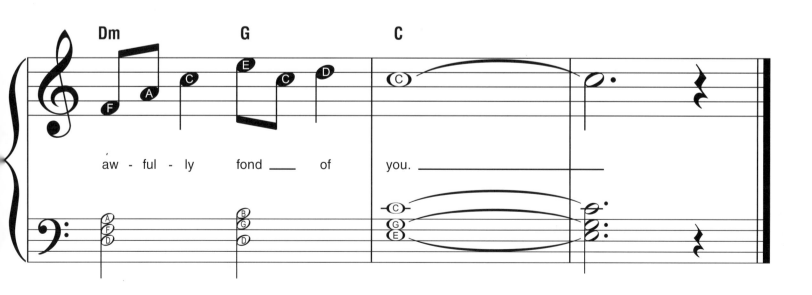

The Rainbow Connection
from THE MUPPET MOVIE

Words and Music by Paul Williams
and Kenneth L. Ascher

Moderately

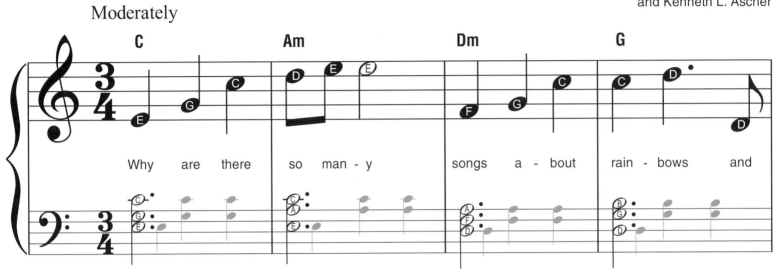

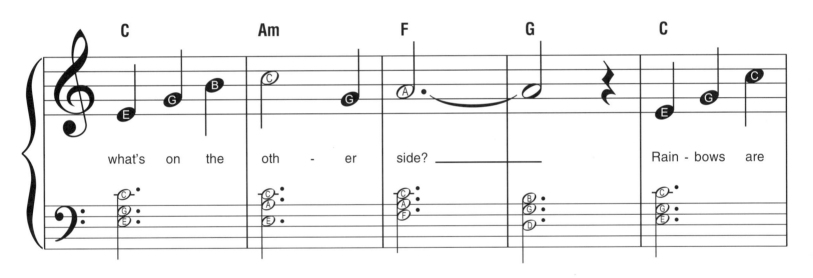

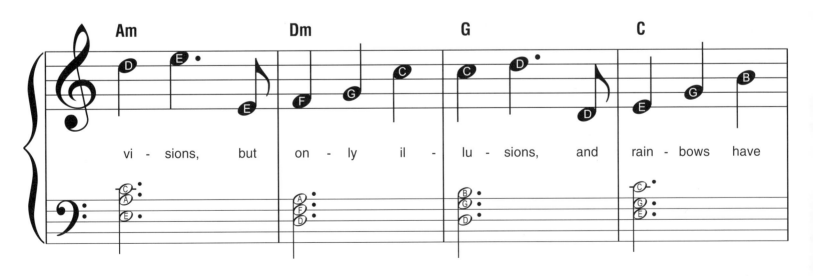

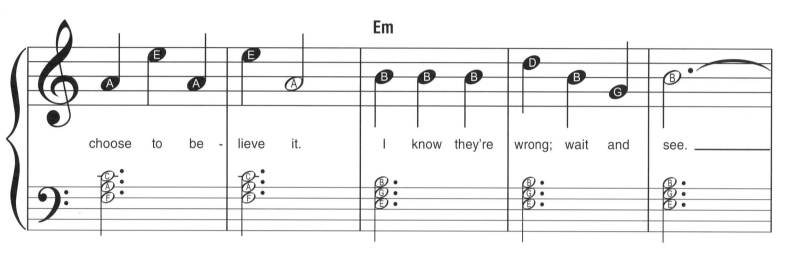

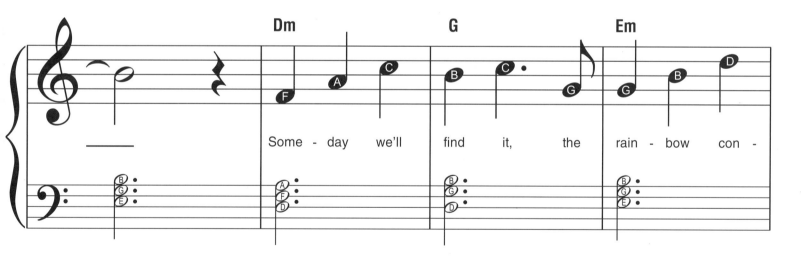

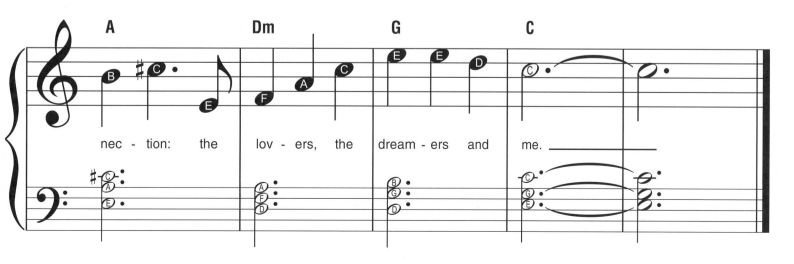

Sesame Street Theme
from the Television Series SESAME STREET

Words by Bruce Hart,
Jon Stone and Joe Raposo
Music by Joe Raposo

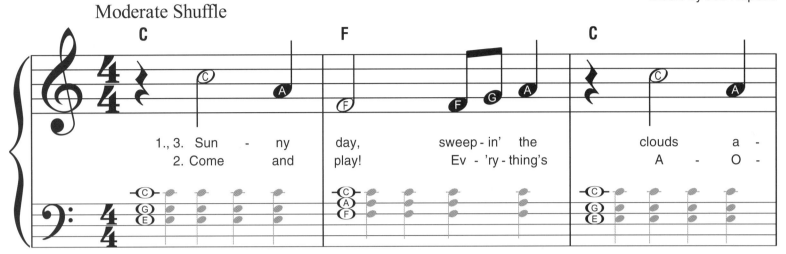

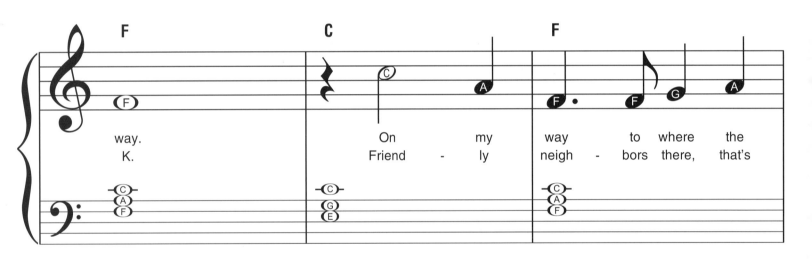

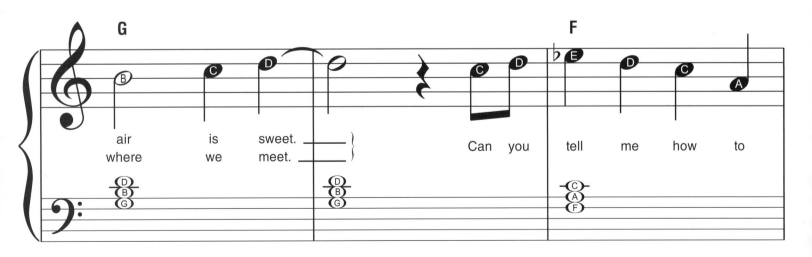

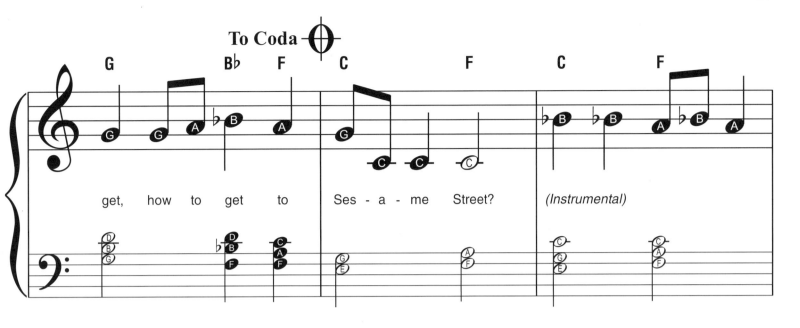

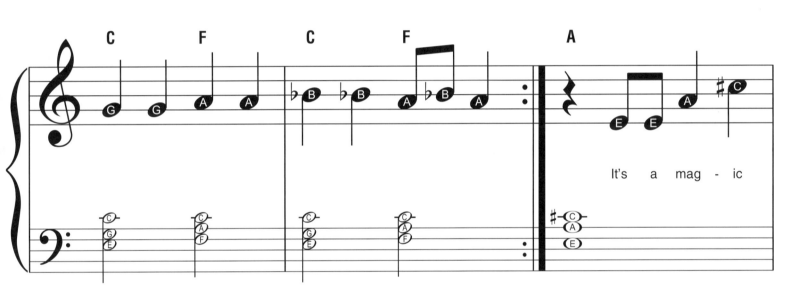

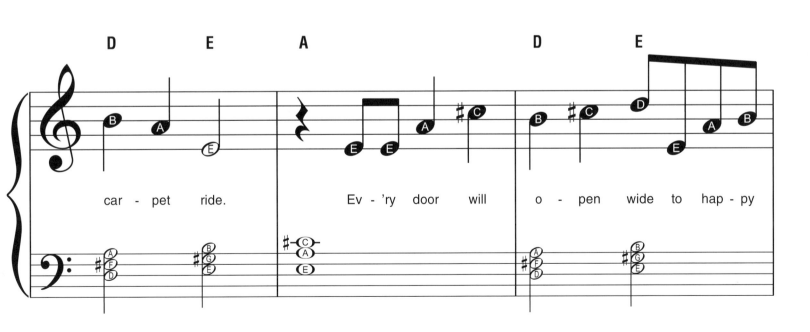

58

D.C. al Coda
(Return to beginning,
play to ⊕ and skip to Coda)

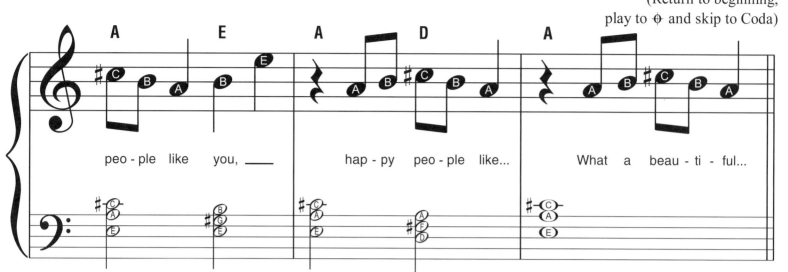

peo - ple like you, ____   hap - py peo - ple like...   What a beau - ti - ful...

CODA

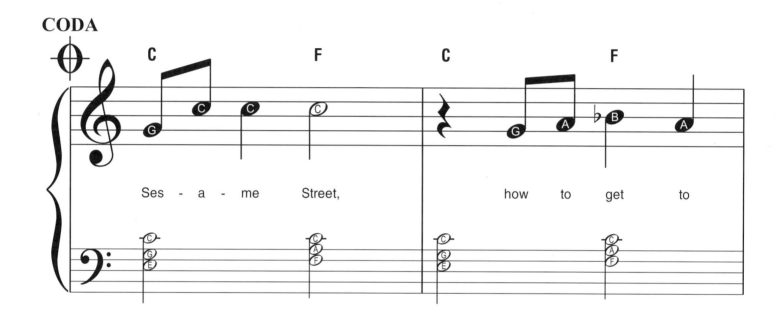

Ses - a - me Street,   how to get to

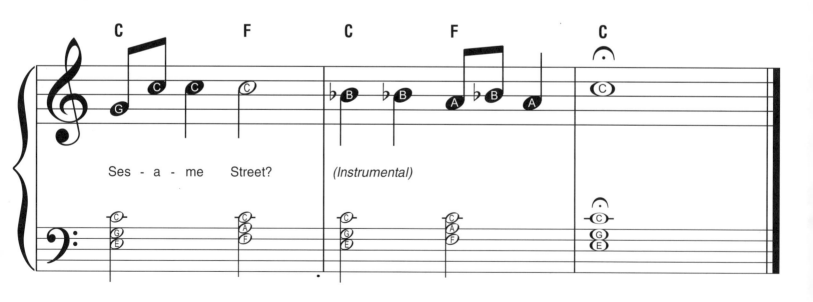

Ses - a - me Street?   *(Instrumental)*

Sing
from SESAME STREET

Words and Music by
Joe Raposo

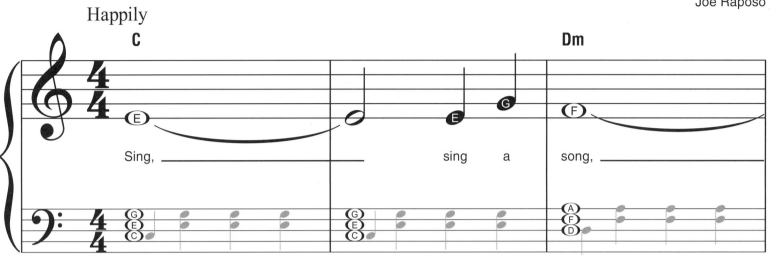

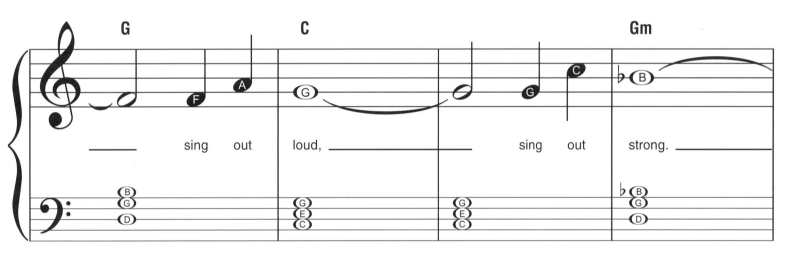

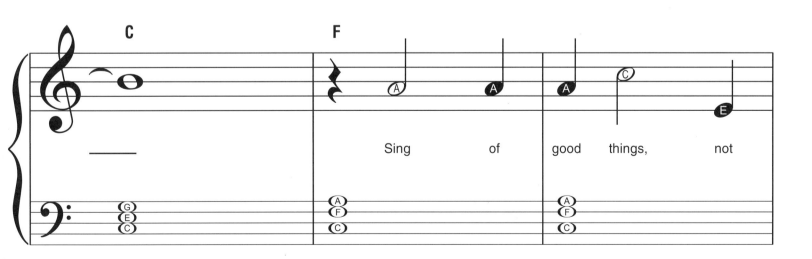

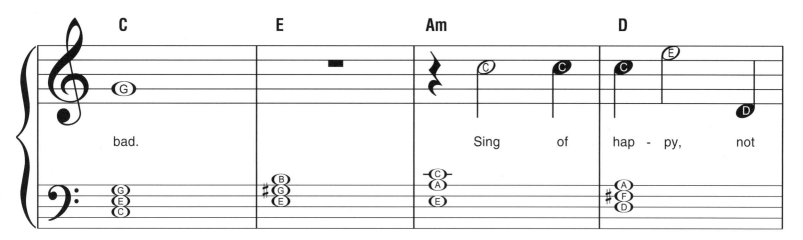

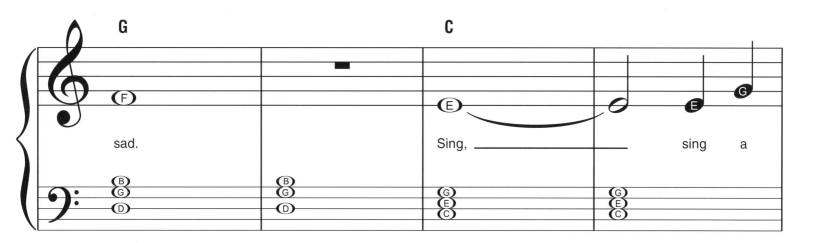

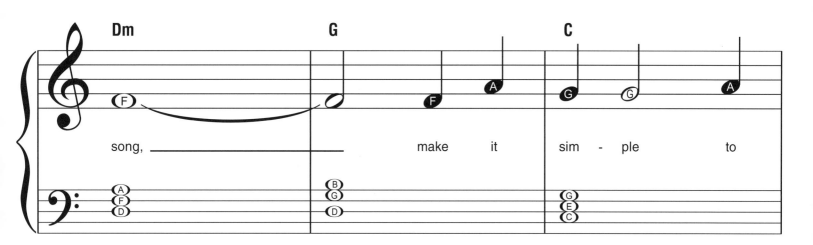

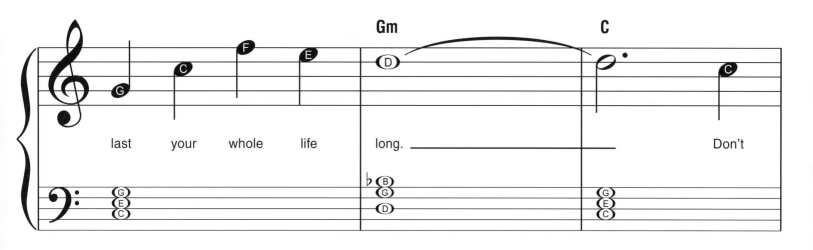

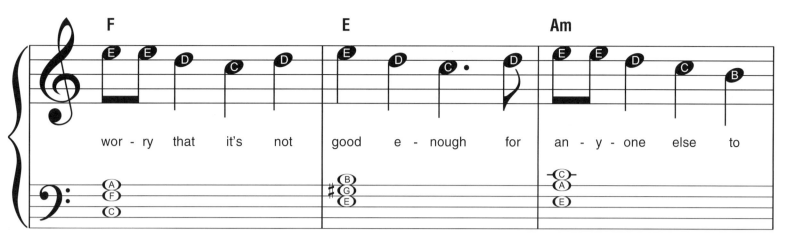

wor - ry that it's not good e - nough for an - y - one else to

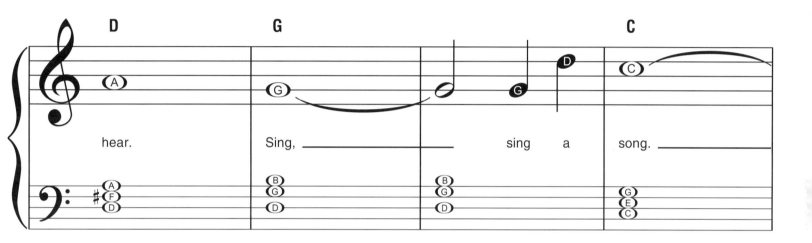

hear. Sing, ___ sing a song. ___

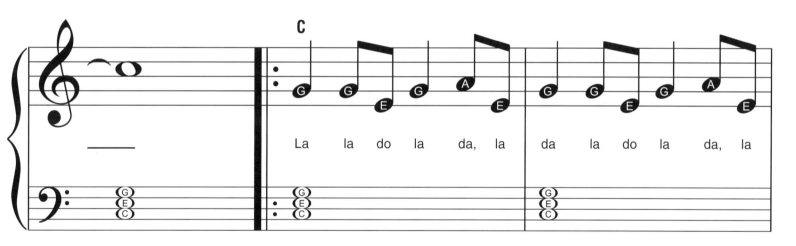

___ La la do la da, la da la do la da, la

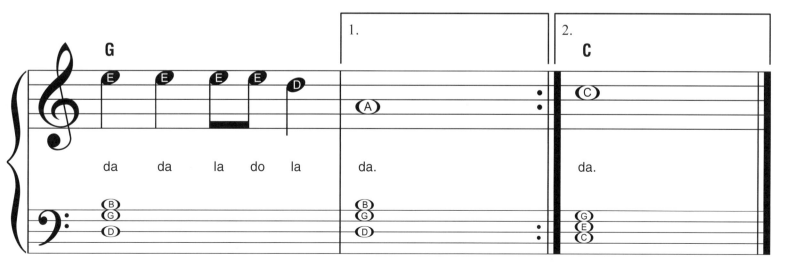

da da la do la da. da.

SpongeBob SquarePants
Theme Song

from SPONGEBOB SQUAREPANTS

Words and Music by Mark Harrison,
Blaise Smith, Steve Hillenburg
and Derek Drymon

Moderate Shuffle

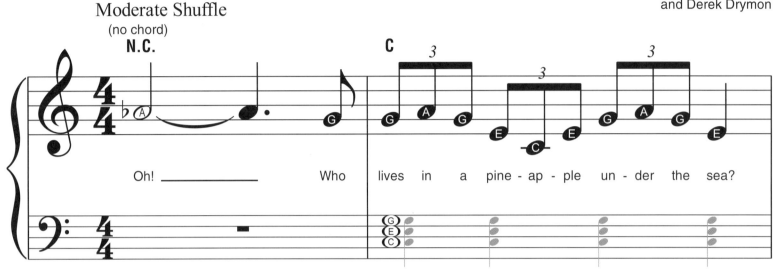

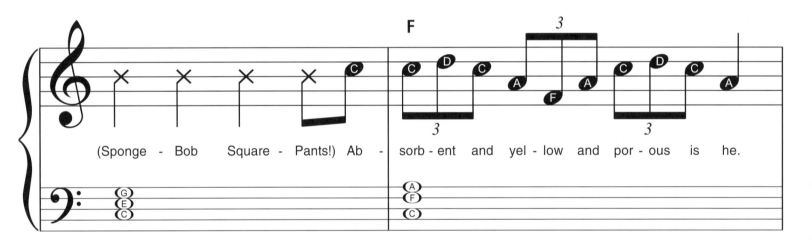

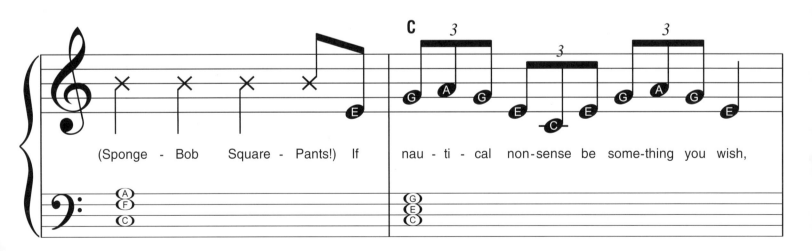

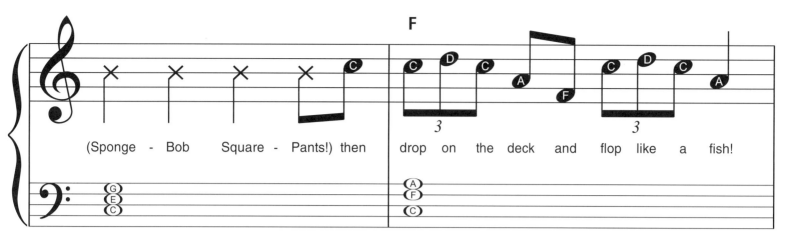

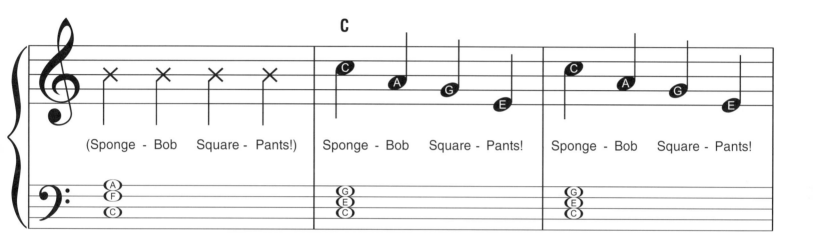

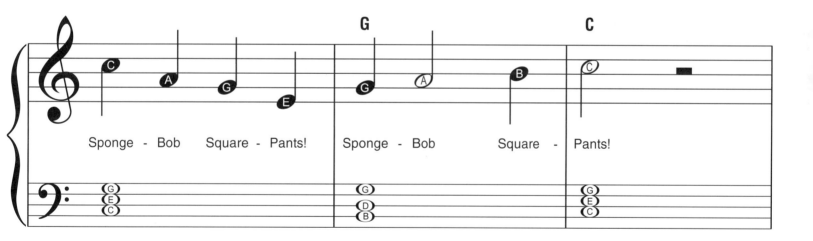

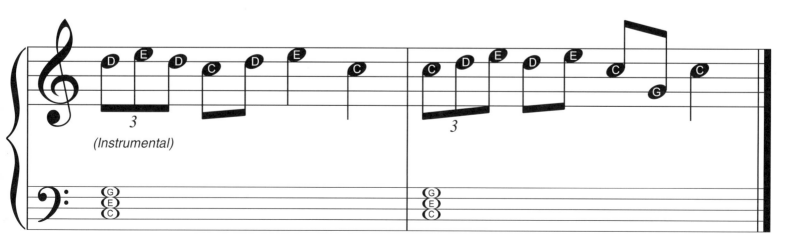

Take Me Out to the Ball Game

Words by Jack Norworth
Music by Albert von Tilzer

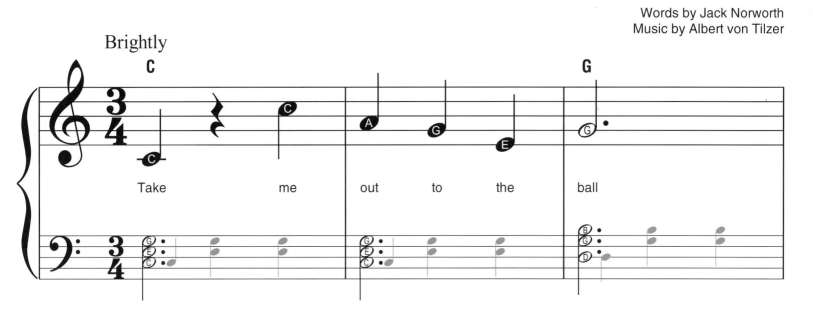

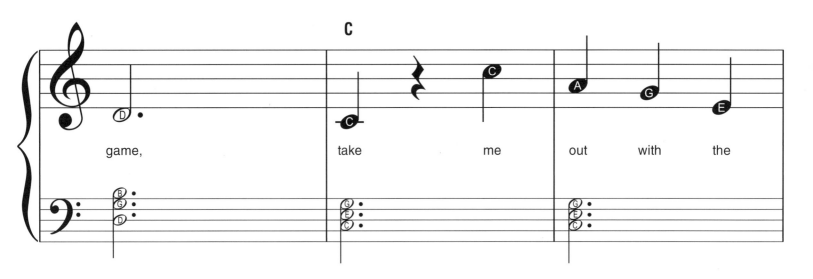

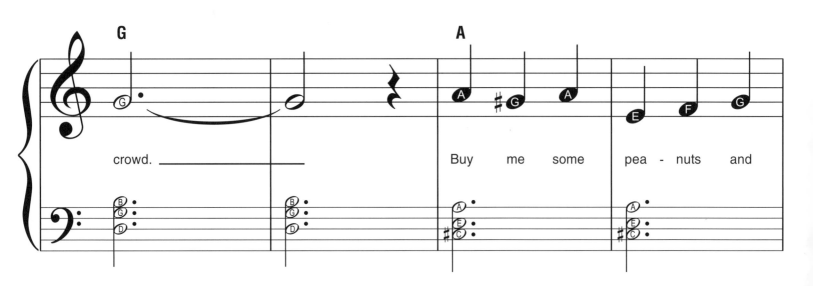

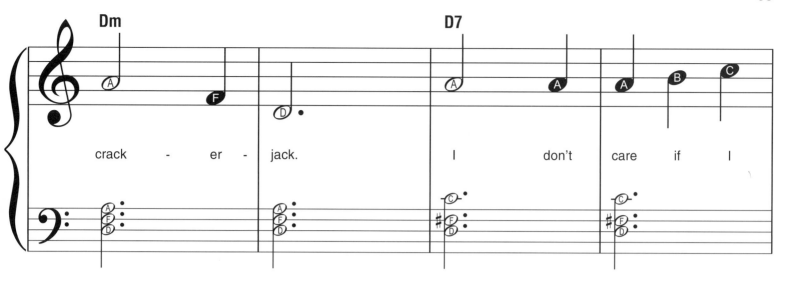

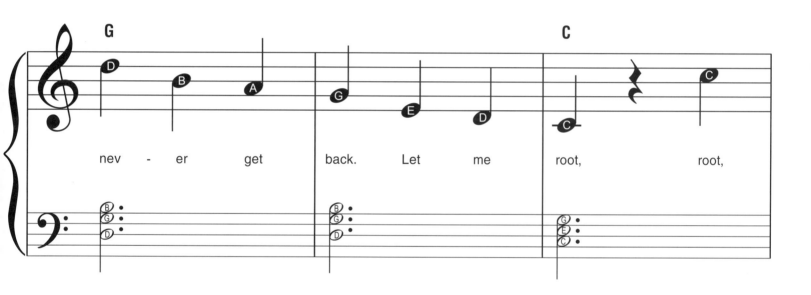

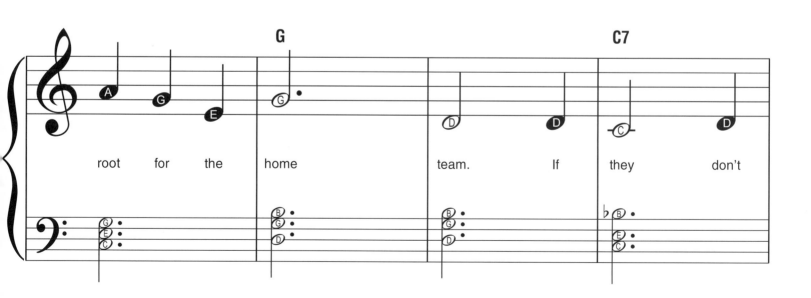

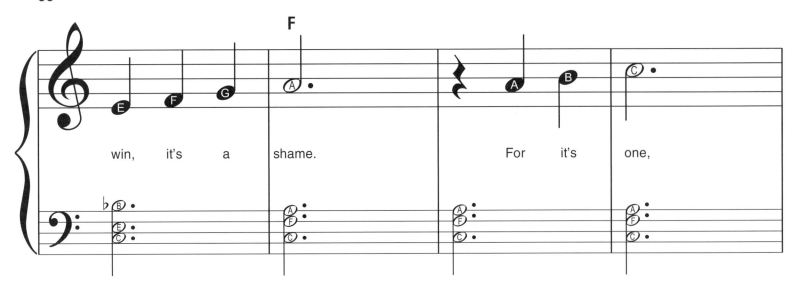

win, it's a shame.   For it's one,

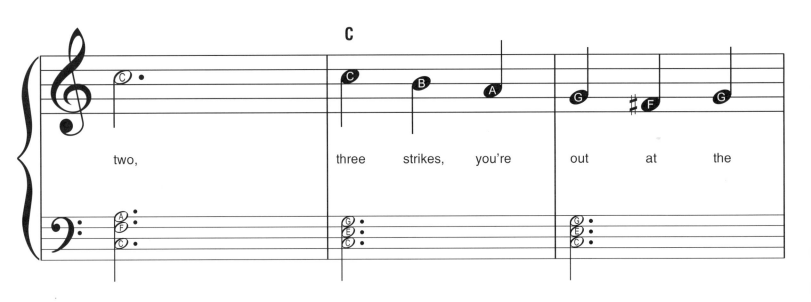

two,   three strikes, you're   out at the

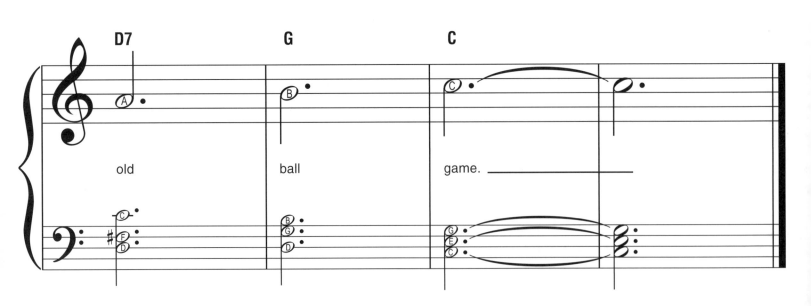

old   ball   game. _____

Tomorrow
from the Musical Production ANNIE

Lyric by Martin Charnin
Music by Charles Strouse

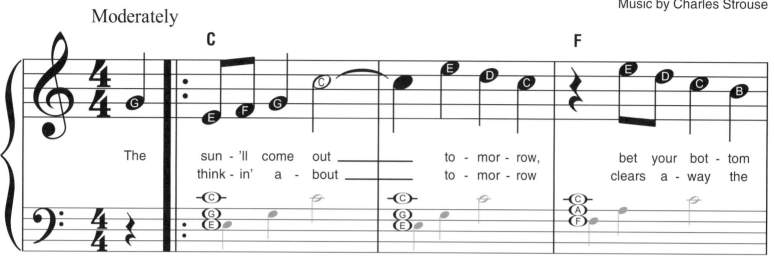

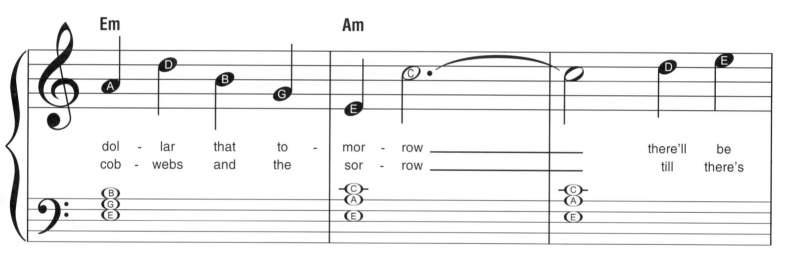

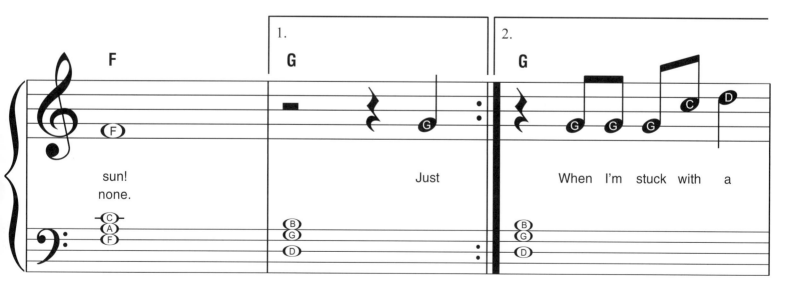

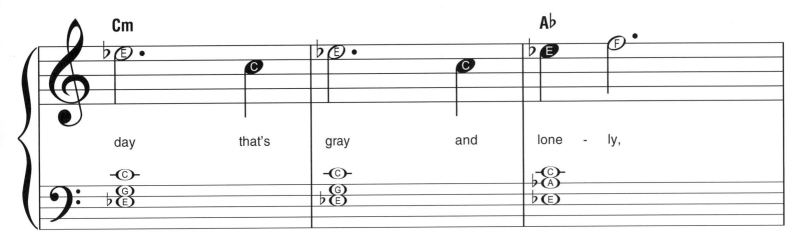

day   that's   gray   and   lone - ly,

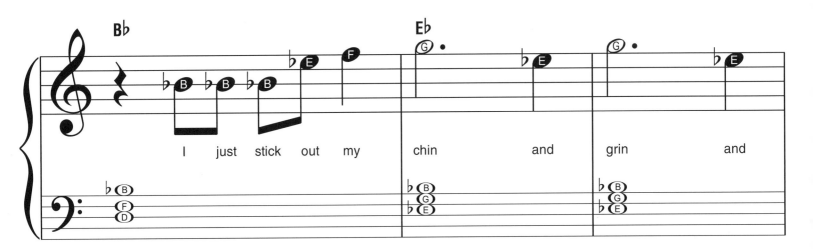

I   just   stick   out   my   chin   and   grin   and

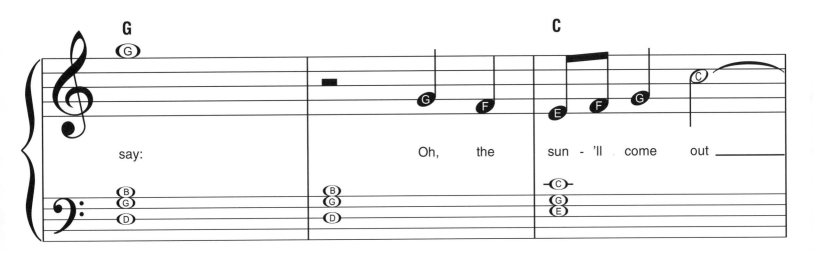

say: Oh,   the   sun - 'll   come   out _____

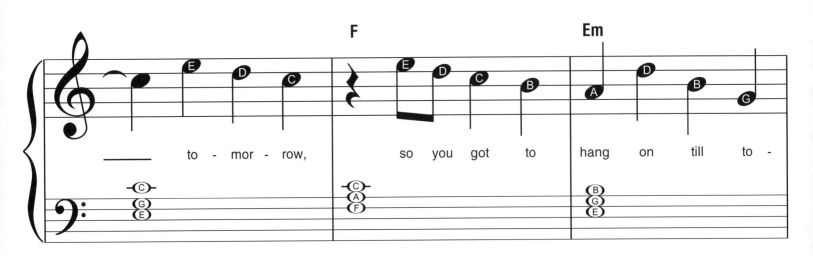

_____ to - mor - row,   so   you   got   to   hang   on   till   to -

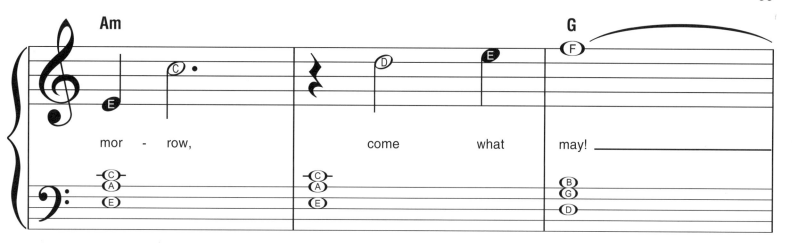

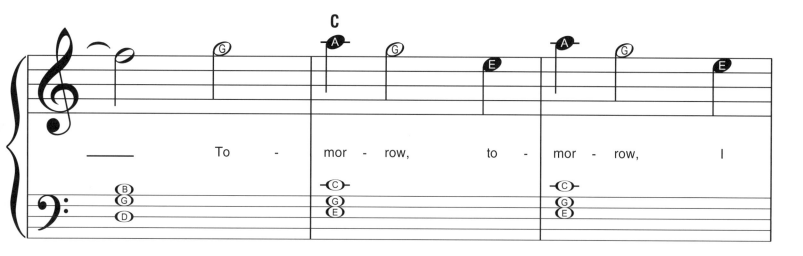

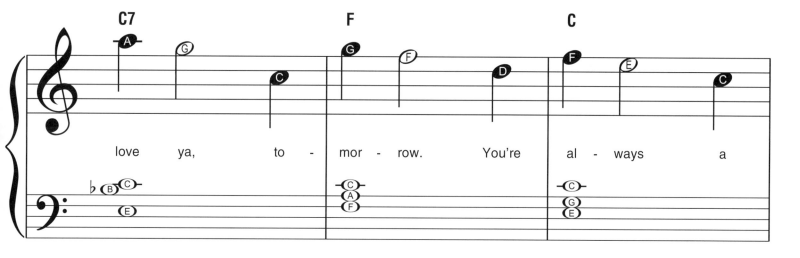

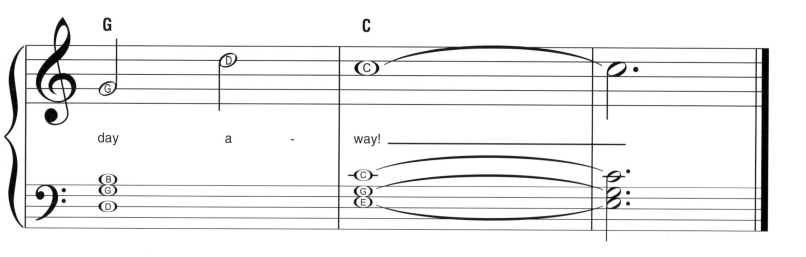

Twinkle, Twinkle Little Star

Traditional

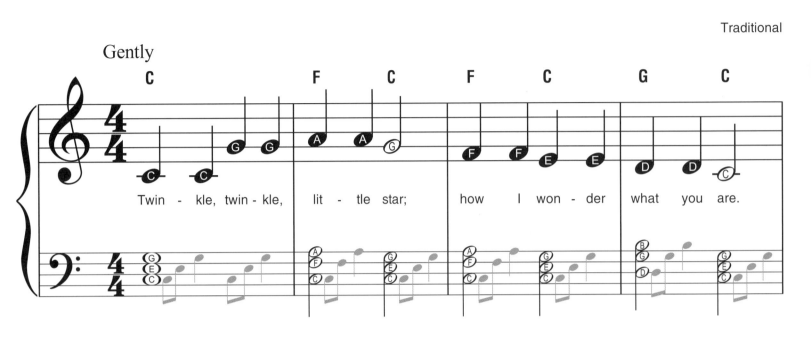

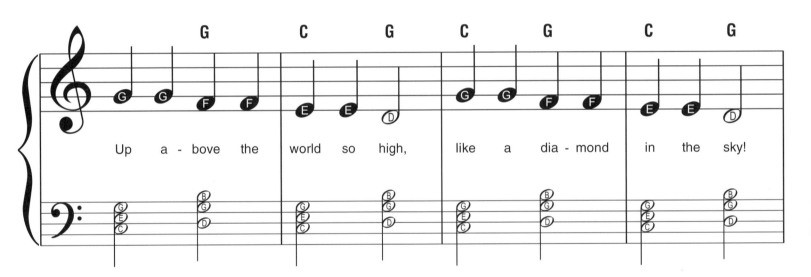

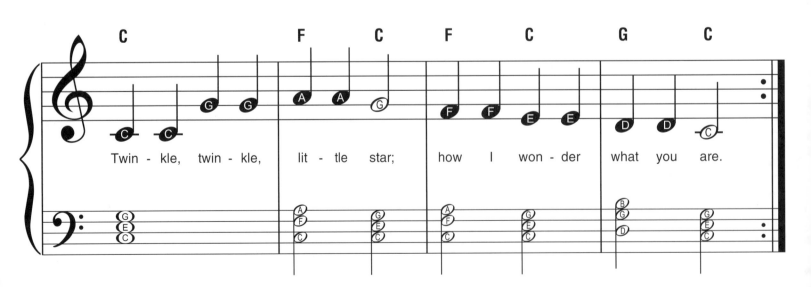

Warm Kitty

featured on the CBS Television Show THE BIG BANG THEORY

Music adapted from an English Folk Tune by
Laura Pendleton MacCarteney
Lyrics by Edith Newlin

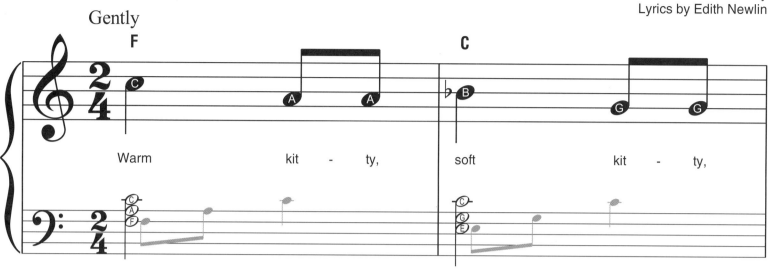

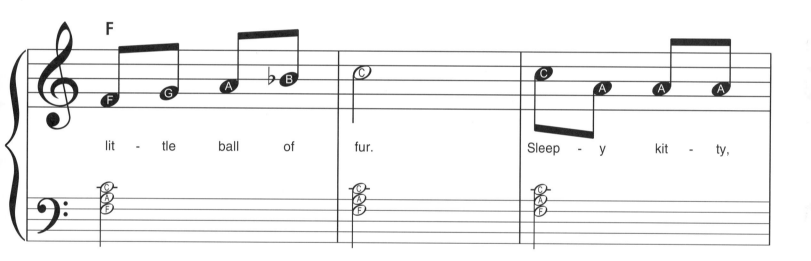

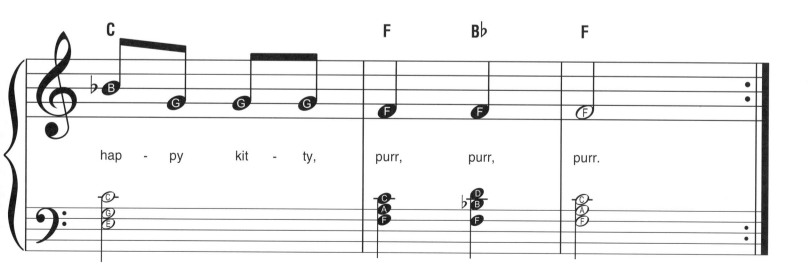

The Wheels on the Bus

Traditional

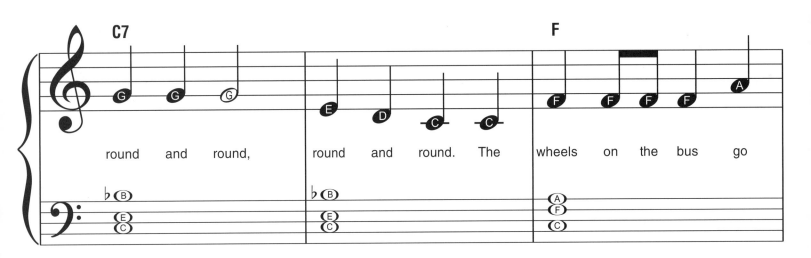

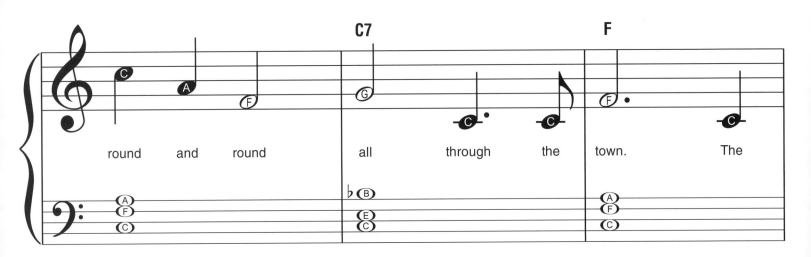

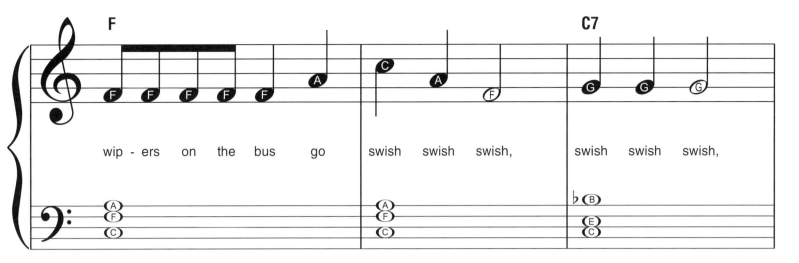

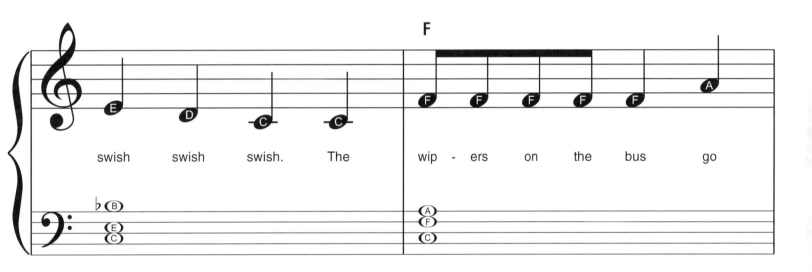

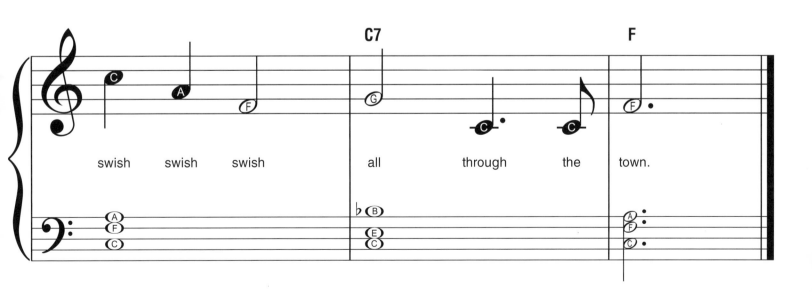

You Are My Sunshine

Words and Music by
Jimmie Davis

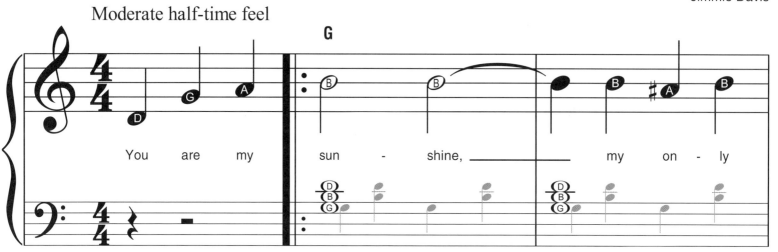

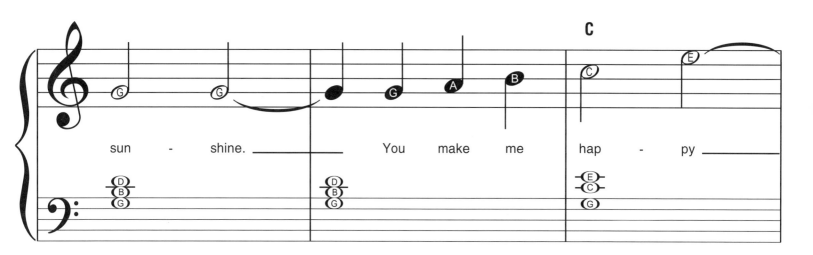

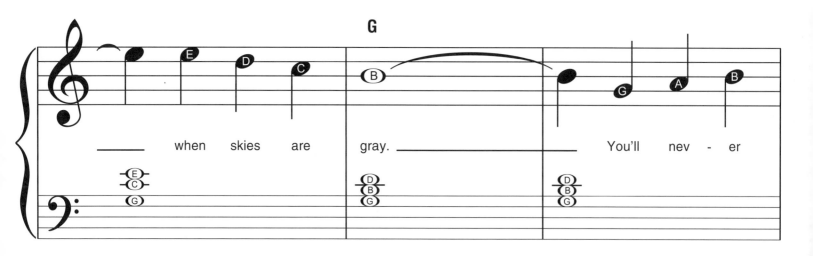

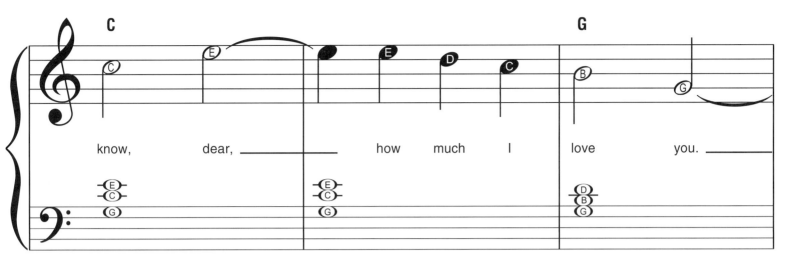

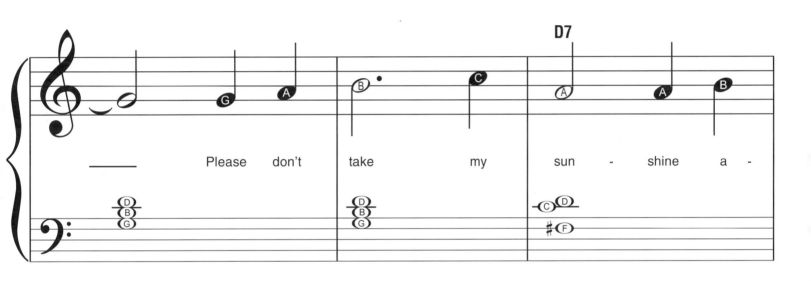

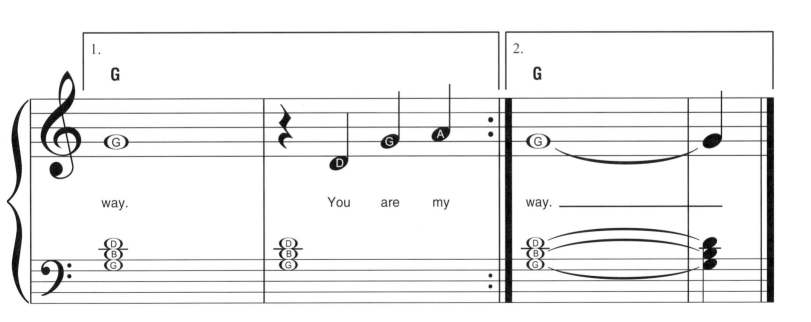

Won't You Be My Neighbor?
(It's a Beautiful Day in the Neighborhood)
from MISTER ROGER'S NEIGHBORHOOD

Words and Music by
Fred Rogers

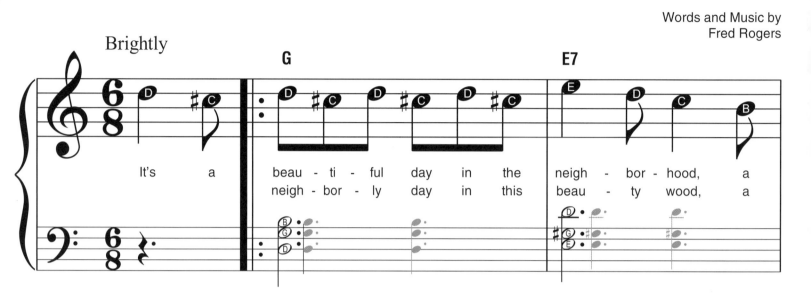

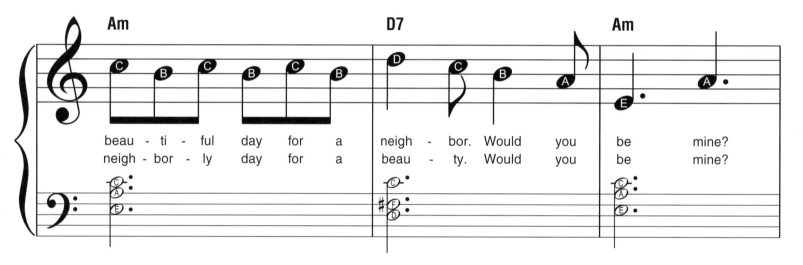

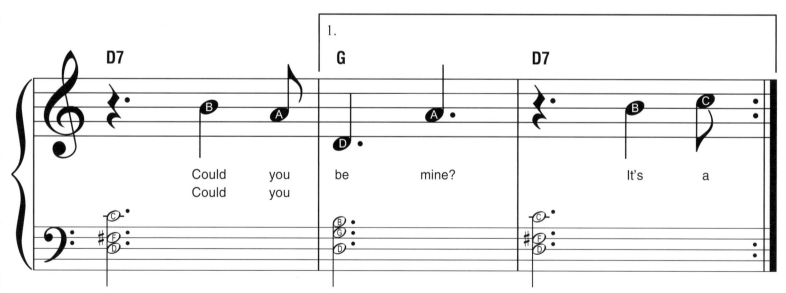

INSTANT Piano Songs

The **Instant Piano Songs** series will help you play your favorite songs quickly and easily—whether you use one hand or two! Start with the melody in your right hand, adding basic left-hand chords when you're ready. Letter names inside each note speed up the learning process, and optional rhythm patterns take your playing to the next level. Online backing tracks are also included. Stream or download the tracks using the unique code inside each book, then play along to build confidence and sound great!

THE BEATLES
All My Loving • Blackbird • Can't Buy Me Love • Eleanor Rigby • Get Back • Here, There and Everywhere • Hey Jude • I Will • Let It Be • Michelle • Nowhere Man • Ob-La-Di, Ob-La-Da • Penny Lane • When I'm Sixty-Four • With a Little Help from My Friends • Yesterday • and more.
00295926 Piano Solo $14.99

CHRISTMAS STANDARDS
All I Want for Christmas Is You • Christmas Time Is Here • Frosty the Snow Man • Grown-Up Christmas List • A Holly Jolly Christmas • I'll Be Home for Christmas • Jingle Bell Rock • The Little Drummer Boy • Mary, Did You Know? • Merry Christmas, Darling • Rudolph the Red-Nosed Reindeer • White Christmas • and more.
00294854 Piano Solo $14.99

CLASSICAL THEMES
Canon (Pachelbel) • Danube Waves (Ivanovici) • Für Elise (Beethoven) • Impromptu, Op. 142, No. 2 (Schubert) • Jesu, Joy of Man's Desiring (Bach) • Jupiter (Holst) • Lullaby (Brahms) • Pomp and Circumstance (Elgar) • The Sleeping Beauty Waltz (Tchaikovsky) • Spring (Vivaldi) • Symphony No. 9, Fourth Movement ("Ode to Joy") (Beethoven) • To a Wild Rose (MacDowell) • Trumpet Voluntary (Clarke) • William Tell Overture (Rossini) • and more.
00283826 Easy Piano Solo $14.99

DISNEY FAVORITES
Beauty and the Beast • Can You Feel the Love Tonight • Chim Chim Cher-ee • Colors of the Wind • A Dream Is a Wish Your Heart Makes • Friend like Me • How Far I'll Go • It's a Small World • Kiss the Girl • Lava • Let It Go • Mickey Mouse March • Part of Your World • Reflection • Remember Me (Ernesto de la Cruz) • A Whole New World • You'll Be in My Heart (Pop Version) • and more.
00283720 Easy Piano Solo $14.99

MOVIE SONGS
As Time Goes By • City of Stars • Endless Love • Hallelujah • I Will Always Love You • Laura • Moon River • My Heart Will Go on (Love Theme from 'Titanic') • Over the Rainbow • Singin' in the Rain • Skyfall • Somewhere Out There • Stayin' Alive • Tears in Heaven • Unchained Melody • Up Where We Belong • The Way We Were • What a Wonderful World • and more.
00283718 Easy Piano Solo $14.99

POP HITS
All of Me • Chasing Cars • Despacito • Feel It Still • Havana • Hey, Soul Sister • Ho Hey • I'm Yours • Just Give Me a Reason • Love Yourself • Million Reasons • Perfect • Riptide • Shake It Off • Stay with Me • Thinking Out Loud • Viva La Vida • What Makes You Beautiful • and more.
00283825 Easy Piano Solo $14.99

www.halleonard.com

It's super easy! This series features accessible arrangements for piano, with simple right-hand melody, letter names inside each note, and basic left-hand chord diagrams. Perfect for players of all ages!

THE BEATLES
00198161..$14.99

BROADWAY
00193871..$14.99

JOHNNY CASH
00287524 ....$9.99

CHRISTMAS CAROLS
00277955 ....$14.99

CHRISTMAS SONGS
00236850 ....$14.99

CLASSICAL
00194693..$14.99

COUNTRY
00285257..$14.99

DISNEY
00199558..$14.99

FOUR CHORD SONGS
00249533 ....$14.99

GOSPEL
00285256..$14.99

HIT SONGS
00194367..$14.99

HYMNS
A00194659..$14.99

JAZZ STANDARDS
00233687..$14.99

ELTON JOHN
00298762 ....$9.99

KIDS' SONGS
00198009..$14.99

THE LION KING
00303511 ....$9.99

ANDREW LLOYD WEBBER
00249580 ....$14.99

MOVIE SONGS
00233670..$14.99

POP STANDARDS
00233770..$14.99

QUEEN
00294889..$9.99

ED SHEERAN
00287525..$9.99

THREE CHORD SONGS
00249664 ....$14.99

TOP HITS
00300405 ....$9.99

HAL•LEONARD®
WWW.HALLEONARD.COM

Prices, contents and availability subject to change without notice.
Disney Characters and Artwork TM & © 2019 Disney

0819
327